THE LEGACY
OF
TUTANKHAMUN
ART AND HISTORY

MEY ZAKI
FARID ATIYA PRESS

THE LEGACY
OF
TUTANKHAMUN
ART AND HISTORY

MEY ZAKI

FARID ATIYA PRESS

**The Legacy
of
Tutankhamun
Art and History**

Text by Mey Zaki
Photographs by Farid Atiya

Published by Abydos Publications
Farid Atiya Press
© Farid Atiya Press
First Edition 2008

P. O. Box 75, 6th of October City, Giza, Egypt
www.abydospublications.com

Colour Seperation by Farid Atiya Press
Printed and bound in Egypt by Farid Atiya Press

Dar el-Kuteb Registration 16169 / 2007
ISBN 977-17-4930-7

Previous Page : Limestone statue of Tutankhamun as god Amun, Luxor Museum.

TABLE OF CONTENTS

Left : Tutankhamun as god Khonsu, Cairo Museum.
Next page : Recumbent statuette of Tutankhamun (see page 62).

HISTORY OF TUTANKHAMUN
AND
HIS FAMILY

Howard Carter and Lord Carnarvon entered the tomb of Tutankhamun on November 27, 1922, they found themselves facing a storehouse of antiquities and luxury, Carter knew the meaning of the solar disk whose rays ended in hands present on the back of the throne, but it was surprising to find it on a piece of furniture belonging to King Tutankhamun, who had restored the old religion in Thebes.

To better understand the situation, we must return to a time when Egyptian power was reaching its peak and civilization appeared in all fields: sculpture, painting, metalwork and reliefs. This development took place after the numerous, successful military campaigns by 18th Dynasty kings in Asia and Nubia. Linked by relationships and alliances, Egypt's neighbours never dreamed of invasion, instead every year they sent gifts to Egypt accompanied by letters of friendship.

The fact that Egypt was the head of an Asian empire affected the country on several levels especially religious and artistic. Military men, shopkeepers, prisoners of war and immigrants brought with them a lot of ideas, traditions, religions and deities, which were susceptible to be partially or fully integrated into the Egyptian civilization. The change in mentality led to a change in the religion, which was dedicated to the sun, to another concept based on the worship of the sun-like star called Aten, who later became the sole object of worship.

This cult began under Thutmosis IV (1400-1390 BC) and flourished under his son Amenhotep III (1390-1352 BC), when dignitaries added references to Aten in the hymns to the sun, and through his wife Queen Tiye who had great influence on the history of Egypt and on the life of her son Amenhotep IV (Akhenaten). This cult developed over time to achieve its final form, and name (The cult of Aten).

He was the second son of Amenhotep III and Tiye, his elder brother Thutmosis V died prematurely. He began his reign during his father's lifetime due to a disease that attacked the latter and took full power upon his death (in 1352 BC). During the first five years of his reign, Amenhotep IV conformed to Egyptian tradition, he was crowned in the temple of Amun at Karnak like his father, took the name Amenhotep IV and built large buildings in honour of Amun-Ra in Karnak. However, he soon changed his name to Akhenaten and built a temple, which diverged from classic Egyptian temples in both its plan and its decoration.

Akhenaten married a woman of royal blood named Nefertiti four years after his ascension to the throne, who had as her title: (The great royal wife), she was the daughter of Ay, a divine father and royal secretary, born in the ninth nome of Upper Egypt. Nefertiti played a more important role in politics than was usual, she dominates the scenes carved on the blocks of the temple of the god. Akhenaten had six daughters with Nefertiti, whose names are: Meritaten, Maketaten, Ankhsenpaaten, Nefernefruaten Ta-sherit, Nefernefrure and Setepenre. He married the first three, but only the eldest Meritaten was placed on the throne and named a 'royal' wife after her mother left the political scene. As for Ankhsenpaaten, she afterwards became the wife of Tutankhamun.

Akhenaten was also married to Princess Tadukhepa (the daughter of an ally Tushratta of Mitanni), who had recently arrived at the court to marry his father Amenhotep III before his illness. And following year 12 of Akhenaten's reign, an unknown woman called Kiya was represented next to him during festivities. She was elevated to that position because she bore the titles: "Greatly beloved wife of the King of Upper and Lower Egypt, the beautiful child of the god Aten, who lives in truth forever."

In year 14 of Akhenaten's reign, Queen Tiye died and was probably buried in the royal necropolis at Tell el-Amarna, because of the absence of her mourning scene in Thebes. A scene in the royal tomb of Akhenaten in Tell el-Amarna shows the royal couple in the process of crying for one of the daughters, who had died in childbirth. Next to the couple a wet nurse is standing with a baby, the child's father was probably Akhenaten and the toddler could be Tutankhamun.

After the death of this princess, there are no more pictures of Queen Nefertiti, perhaps she fell into disgrace, or had ceased to share the king's ideas and had withdrawn some distance to the region north of the

Left : The face of the Tutankhamun, Middle coffin (see page 36).

city. In year 17 Nefertiti died in her turn and Meritaten, the beloved daughter aged 13, was associated with her father. In a letter from el-Amarna, she carries the qualities of (Mistress of the King's house) and (Great royal wife).

The country's administration was not handled by Akhenaten, who was dedicated to his god, so civil and military authority fell under the control of two strong personalities, Ay the divine father and Horemheb the military general, and both would become pharaohs at the end of the 18th Dynasty.

During the reign of Akhenaten, Egypt lived under a strong authority, the inscriptions of the god Amun were destroyed countrywide, wherever that name appeared on buildings, stelae or carved obelisks, it was erased and pounded away, which proves the authority of the officials used to carry out this mission.

Everything changed at the end of Akhenaten's reign when he wished to be reconciled with the priesthood of Amun and sent his daughter and son-in-law Semenkhkare to Thebes, but it was too late to create a good relationship with the priests. After the death of Akhenaten during year 18 of his reign, he was certainly buried in his royal tomb, because of the royal seal that can be found on the door of the funerary chamber. However, Egyptologists think that Akenhaten's mummy was hidden and kept in the Valley of the Kings by his followers, where his adversaries could never find it.

The Tell el-Amarna letters are clay tablets containing letters and dispatches sent by vassal states written in Akkadian, which was the diplomatic language of the time. In these letters that survived the destruction of Akhenaten's objects, there were complaints about the pharaoh's neglect of them, revealing the problems they were facing, especially threats presented by powerful nations. The weakness of Egypt and its absence from the political scene at the time pushed former enemies to attack their neighbours.

Thus at the time of his death Akhenaton left a weak and fragile country, it required an iron fist to keep authority and stability and restore power on Egypt's borders and in the eastern cities. To ensure continuity, King Akhenaten had appointed a king before his death, a co-regent who has not been identified with certainty called Nefernefruaten (Smenkhkare), he died after a short reign (circa 1336 BC).

A young pharaoh eight years of age named Tutankhamun succeeded him, his ties to the royal family conferred legitimacy on his occupation of the throne. He reinforced his political position by marrying the Princess Ankhesenpaaten, the third daughter of Akhenaten and Nefertiti born in Thebes, before her father moved the capital to Akhetaten. Ankhesenpaaten would have been ten years older than her young husband, she was one of the three daughters, who married their father Akhenaten and she would have been able to give good advice to Tutankhamun. After ten years when her husband died at the age of eighteen, she turned out to have a very independent mind.

Right : Statue of the goddess Sekhmet (see page 66).

AKHENATEN'S CAPITAL AKHETATEN

The religious climate of Egypt at that time was one of tension, and there could be no peaceful coexistence between the two religions, but the suppression of the former cult could not destroy ancient beliefs and the situation became unbearable in the capital. Amenhotep IV's belief in the god Aten, the only creator of the universe was developed over time.

Akhenaten thought that the cult of the god needed to be celebrated in a virgin place and during year 6 of his reign when he changed his name to Akhenaten, he chose a new capital in Middle Egypt 350 kilometres north of Thebes. It was a site in the 15th nome of Luxor, halfway between Memphis and Thebes, located between the hills on the eastern bank of the Nile that he called the (Horizon of Aten), which included a large agricultural area of more than 240 square kilometres west of the Nile, able to sustain a population of about 50,000 inhabitants. Akhenaten surrounded this capital with 14 stelae (called frontier stelae) with engraved inscriptions to delineate its borders and establish the principles of the royal family's life.

This site contained: The northern palace and two southern palaces on the western side, the house of jubilation, in the city centre: the daytime palace of the king and his family. The first was a royal residence and included courtrooms, reception areas, the ceremonial rooms of the royal family and a vast vineyard. The second was an executive palace where Akhenaten worked and at the same time it was a liturgical building, within these edifices were large courtyards and pools planted with trees. The rooms where the king resided with his family were decorated with paintings of nature and sometimes the royal family. These palaces were surrounded by administrative offices.

The area of the necropolis included: a civil part for priests and officials and the royal necropolis. The notables of Amarna are known by their tombs: Nakht vizier of the south, General Ramose, Ranefer director of the stables, Ay the divine father and husband of Nefertiti's wet-nurse. The tombs belonging to the king's faithful servants are on the east side for topographical reasons. None of the dignitaries' tombs have been used, and few were occupied. All the pictures represent royal scenes of the king and his wife in the palace.

This capital that Akhenaten called (the horizon of Aten) or Tell el-Amarna became the favourite place of the king and his family, where they could promote and serve their god Aten through hymns containing the essence of the new theology.

The city of Akhetaten was certainly beautiful with its villas, palaces and gardens. The few remains give an idea of the beauty of the palace's decoration and the new naturalistic style of decoration. The artists mastered this new style and were able to create works of incomparable beauty in sculpture. Life in Akhetaten was idyllic and this was the fixed aim of King Akhenaten, but the city was devastated and abandoned, and its stones used in other buildings afterwards. Sand covered the palaces, villas, gardens, workshops and the city fell into oblivion following the collapse of the religion of Aten.

Left : Statue of Akhenaten.
Overleaf, left : Unfinished head of Nefertiti.
Overleaf, right : Panel with adoration scene of Aten.

THE ATEN CULT

The new worship seemed to have been made for Akhenaten and his family, from the multitude of kings he kept only the sun, the motivating power of the world, the physical manifestation of a higher authority. All that was not life was expunged and night was the time of all types of peril. This monotheism was of a particular kind since it was accessible only to the royal family.

The relationship between Akhenaten and Aten was one between father and son, the king was the intermediary between the people and the god. This cult was centred on the worship of the god Aten, of which all life should be fearful, in accordance with the Egyptian principle of Maat, which played an important role in the unfolding of existence in Egypt, and this signified living under a strict discipline.

The great hymn addressed to the god Aten, was the work of King Akhenaten, it describes the beneficial and universal action of the star and reveals elements that allow some understanding of the cult. The most complete version can be found in the tomb of Ay (the head of the king's horses), high priest of Akhenaten and Tutankhamun, who later succeeded Tutankhamun. By looking at the contents of the Aten hymns, we realize that the tributes paid to him can be found in older ones addressed to other Egyptian gods and more particularly to the god Ra. These hymns are not the worship of Aten, Akhenaten and the queen, but of Aten by Akhenaten and the queen.

THE ATEN ART

The most visible part of the genius of Akhenaten is certainly his new concept of art and particularly its completely unexpected application to the human form. It is a liberation of forms, which deviates from realism without actually abandoning it.

Akhenaton led Egypt during a revolutionary period and a new artistic style. For the first time in Egyptian history finesse was rejected, the human form was more schematic with certain details exaggerated. For portraits, the court adopted quite unusual physical characteristics for the king and the young princesses, although his wife was not totally subjected to the same deformations.

The repertoire expanded enormously in the area of daily life, scenes lost all religious appearance, but were dominated by the radiant sun god. In all the scenes of King Akhenaten, he appears with his wife and some of their six daughters. The royal couple are sometimes depicted in informal scenes with their daughters on their knees, proving that family members were close and affectionate.

The Aten art emphasized very specific details of the anatomy, it was an anti-idealisation of human beings. Features of the Aten art are: a bloated belly, a kilt descending under the navel, skull malformation, a long extended narrow face, ears with pierced lobes, a fleshy mouth, a long nose, skinny arms, almond-shaped eyes, prominent cheekbones, a large head on a slender neck, excessive fullness of the thighs, enormous hips, skinny legs and sandals on the feet of the statues.

Art during the time of Tutankhamun retained many traces of Akhenaten's originality. The extreme charm of this period comes from the fact that it retained the taste for real detail an almost natural realism, without the distortions of the Amarna style.

REIGN OF THE YOUNG PHARAOH TUTANKHAMUN (1339-1329 BC):

The reign of King Tutankhamun or Tutankhaten as he was known at the beginning of his reign, represents an obscure stage at the end of the 18th Dynasty. We call this period (post-Amarna) and even though the pharaoh grew up within the circle of Akhenaten's family, his kinship to the family has never been established with certainty.

A single reference to Tutankhamun dating to the reign of Akhenaten if on a block of one of the buildings belonging to the great Aten temple at Tell el-Amarna, where we read the following inscription: (The son of the King from his body Tutankhaten). This registration shows that it is possible that Tutankhamun was the son of Akhenaten and one of his wives probably Kiya, who bore the title: (Great wife beloved of the King of Upper and Lower Egypt, beautiful child of the living Aten who will live forever).

Tutankhaten spent his childhood in the royal harem, he married his half-sister Ankhesenpaaten and at the beginning of his reign, they retained those names as is evidenced by the various objects found in his tomb on which Aten has been visibly replaced by Amun when both spouses changed their names to Tutankhamun and Ankhesenamun. The return to the old religion and this change demonstrates the royal couple's reconciliation with the representatives of the former order. The young pharaoh moved his capital from Akhetaten to Thebes from year 2 of his reign as pharaoh, and Aten was relegated to the rank of a rarely mentioned divinity.

Tutankhamun aged nine, was crowned in Memphis under the protection of his advisors, the divine father Ay, general Horemheb and the treasurer Maya, very important and influential people who managed the country's policies on the pharaoh's behalf and took the decisions during his reign.

The original tomb of Akhenaten and his family was prepared in a valley close to Akhetaten, but in the early months of Tutankhamun's reign he was reconciled with the old gods of Egypt and the pharaoh abandoned Akhetaten and returned to Thebes when he reigned for 10 years. When the young pharaoh renounced the former religion, he restored the old traditional worship and began to repair the damage of the Amarna period. His first task as a means to strengthen his legitimacy, was to reinter his father Akhenaten, whose remains were transferred from Tell el-Amarna to a tomb in the Valley of Kings.

King Tutankhamun also brought with him funerary furniture belonging to the royal family in Amarna and mortal remains, which he placed in tomb no. 55 in the Valley of Kings. This furniture belonged to Queen Tiye and Kiya, mother of Tutankhamun, but the remains in a coffin with neither a name nor a face could belong to Akhenaten, father of Tutankhamun.

This tomb in the Valley of the Kings famous for the problems it has caused, was discovered in 1907. It was unfinished and its contents had been damaged by floodwater, especially a coffin with an unknown mummy, whose cartouche was damaged to prevent the deceased from reaching the afterlife. The body was at first attributed to a woman possibly Tiye, but after comparing the skeleton, and the blood group of Tutankhamun, it was assigned to the revolutionary King Akhenaten. Tutankhamun son of Akhenaten wanted to protect the body and hid it from the priests in an unknown grave with the name effaced and the facial features removed. Four canopic jars with viscera were also found In the tomb, three of which are in the Cairo Museum and the fourth in the Metropolitan Museum of New York.

During the reign of Tutankhamun some construction work was carried out, statues and stelae at Karnak and the great colonnaded temple in Luxor, which contains scenes of the *Opet* feast. On a stele called (The restoration stele), erected in year 1 of his reign and built in front of the third pylon of the temple of Amun at Karnak, a text describes the status of the country during the early reign of Tutankhamun and how the young pharaoh had rebuilt the stelae, the shrines and the buildings to please the god. Another inscribed text reads: (Having taken care of the father who had begot him, he reigns under the paternal royalty of Osiris), (Tutankhamun appeared on the paternal throne, and governed the realm of Horus). The same stele also mentions the restoration work carried out by Tutankhamun throughout Egypt on all the monuments mutilated under Akhenaten.

In Thebes the Luxor temple built by Amenhotep III, Akhenaten's father and continued by Ramses II, bears traces of the work accomplished during the years of Tutankhamun's reign. The great entry colonnade was decorated with a series of reliefs with the theme of the annually celebrated *Opet* festival, together with the sacred marriage between Amun-Ra and Amunet. During this celebration the gods and king travelled from the temple at Karnak to that at Luxor by land and river simultaneously, and returned after the festival to Karnak temple at another time. Horemheb's name appears several times on this colonnade as on all of Tutankhamun's monuments, as he replaced Tutankhamun's name with his own, but the original name is clear in some areas.

The king died young in the ninth year of his reign at the age of 18. According to the medical analysis of his mummy, death was probably due to an accident or fall from a chariot, after breaking a small bone in the cranial cavity. Tutankhamun's successor appears to have been his wife Ankhsenamun in the beginning, because she was the last living member of Akhenaten's family. Tutankhamun's widow was left in a difficult situation as she was surrounded by very ambitious men older than herself. She tried to save her legacy and to remain on the throne of her ancestors, but she made a big mistake by contacting the king of the Hittite empire and revealing the situation saying that her husband was dead and that he himself had many sons and asked for one of these Zannanza, as a husband to ensure the continuity of the royal family. This affair is known from a letter now in Turkey. The prince was assassinated before his arrival in Egypt, probably on the orders of Horemheb, who had during Tutankhamun's reign acted as (general-in-chief, represented the king and was grand chamberlain, responsible for all work undertaken by the sovereign and high priest).

Ankhsenamun was reduced to uniting herself with the 'divine father Ay' to maintain a presence near the throne, the latter became the Egyptian king for four years; his name appeared with Ankhsenamun on a ring. His ascent to the throne was probably legitimized by marriage with the widowed queen. His reign (1327 -1323 BC) left few traces and his name was effaced by his immediate successor Horemheb, who began a policy of restoration of the whole of Egypt.

DISCOVERY OF THE TOMB

"We have finally made a wonderful discovery in the Valley of the Kings. A magnificent tomb with seals intact. Excavation filled in, awaiting your arrival. Congratulations." Carter.

This is the text of the famous telegram sent by Carter to his employer Lord Carnarvon, after clearing the stairs leading to a sealed door marking the entrance to a tomb on November 4, 1922.

Howard Carter (1874-1939), was the son of a father, who was a genre painter from a family of portraitists, he dreamed of being an artist or a high quality professional, and showed an early love of drawing. At the age of 17 he obtained a modest employment with the Egypt Exploration Fund, which was a private British organization created to finance archaeological excavations in Egypt. Carter who knew about Egyptian antiquities, left England for Egypt in 1891 and was sent to Tell el-Amarna or Akhetaten with Flinders Petrie, a famous archaeologist working in Egypt, a few days after his arrival. He was authorized to draw the Egyptian collections.

In 1892, objects of an unusual style were uncovered in the vicinity of Tell el-Amarna. Carter a boy of 17 began to hear about Akhenaten and the Amarna period, thus began his passion for excavation, and he was presented with his first royal tomb, which was almost certainly that of Akhenaten, probably Tutankhamun's father, carved into the rock between the North and South chapels.

In December 1891, the discovery was announced by the Egyptian Department of Antiquities. This unfinished sombre tomb was a huge disappointment to Carter, different from what he had already seen in Beni Hassan. It contained drawings that were difficult to interpret and among its scenes was an important one of Akhenaten and his wife Nefertari mourning the death of their daughter. And above, the solar disk appearing with its rays ending in hands, this same representation that Carter found on the backrest of Tutankhamun's throne 31 years later.

Carter began to draw sketches of the royal tomb in a very precise manner, and during his time working with Petrie, the latter placed a lot of confidence in him and listened to his points of view. The excavations at Tell el-Amarna remained in Carter's memory, because here he was presented with the Aten art for the first time and discovered its elegance.

In 1899 Carter was appointed chief inspector of antiquities for Upper Egypt, this unexpected promotion occurred because the community of archaeologists had accepted him, thanks to his extraordinary talent in drawing, even though he had not attended a high class university or learned anything about ancient Egypt. The outcome was that he spent six years in Deir el-Bahari with Edward Neville, where he carried out the work of chief artisan and assistant to Neville, the excavation director in charge of rebuilding the great temple of Queen Hatshepsut at Deir el-Bahari. His work was so efficient that Neville recommended him to Gaston Maspero, director-general of the department of antiquities.

Carter was very intelligent and observant. During this period he learned very quickly from his associates, he copied all the hieroglyphic texts even those that had been erased or were difficult to read, thanks to his ability to recognize the signs from a few broken lines. He corrected some of Mariette's publications and completed some texts deciphered by specialists.

During his work at Deir el-Bahari Carter had undertaken excavation of a cave south of the temple of Mentuhotep II Nebhepetra (2055 - 2004 BC), where he found a life-size statue of the king. The grave was discovered when his horse fell in to it, the cavity is called (The horse's tomb).

In December 1899, Carter was given the opportunity to work in complete freedom. He began excavations in Thebes and the tomb of Amenhotep II (1427-1400 BC) was his breakthrough. This tomb was a cachette containing a large number of royal burials and in January 1900, Carter was responsible for transporting these mummies to Cairo. This discovery was his first contact with the Valley of the Kings. but that was not the last time, because this valley figured prominently in his thoughts and dreams.

Carter was convinced that there were hidden tombs in the valley, which had not been looted. He worked in the Valley of the Kings a lot, clearing graves, putting up iron gates and installing interior electricity. With the support of Maspero, he looked for a rich patron able to fund research in the valley. In 1903 an American businessman named Theodore Davis began to finance research in the Valley of the Kings. In January 1903 Carter uncovered his first royal tomb that of the Pharaoh Thutmosis IV (1400-1390 BC) robbed in antiquity, but which contained beautifully coloured reliefs.

Carter began searching for the tomb of Amenhotep I in the heights of Draa Abu el-Naga on the hill overlooking the valley of Deir el-Bahari, in his capacity as chief inspector. But in 1904 Maspero changed the functions of the inspectors of Upper and Lower Egypt, which ended the Carter-Davies collaboration. Carter was not pleased, but he obeyed orders. At the end of 1904, the 30-year-old Carter was transferred to Tanta in the Delta, because of some problems he could not resolve during work at Saqqara.

The tomb of Tuya and Yuya, the parents of Queen Tiye, the mother of King Akhenaten was discovered in the Valley of the Kings. This discovery surprised Carter, because the tomb was magnificent and contained abundant funerary material, the best preserved ever discovered in the Valley of the Kings. This discovery was made by James E. Quibell, the Carter colleague who had exchanged his post as inspector of the North with Carter four months earlier.

In 1905, Carter left the Department of Antiquities after three years during which time he had earned his living accompanying groups of tourists around the archaeological sites. He returned to Thebes and found that Davis had decided to conduct excavations in the Valley of the Kings. Carter joined the work team in 1905 and discovered the tomb of Siptah (Edward R. Ayrton working for Davis discovered this tomb.) In January 1907, the important tomb known as no. 55, used as a cachette for funerary furniture and objects belonging to family members of Akhenaten, was discovered. In 1908 the tomb of Horemheb, the last ruler of the 18th Dynasty was brought to light.

Carter was sure that an intact tomb could exist. In January 1909, a shaft was discovered containing fragments bearing the name of Tutankhamun and that of Ay. The shaft was identified by Davis as the tomb of Tutankhamun, but the elements found there did not confirm this identification.

From 1907 a nobleman named Lord Carnarvon (1866-1923) had appeared in Egypt to lead the excavation of the Theban necropolis. He was an English lord, courteous, well educated, rich, a collector who travelled extensively, and was interested in breeding racehorses, hunting and cars. He had had a terrible car accident and his doctor had advised him to spend the winters in Aswan, and during his regular visits to Egypt, Carnarvon focussed increasingly on Egyptian antiquities.

Convinced of the importance of the excavations and realizing he did not have the background, which would allow him to lead them nor the support of a member of the department of antiquities, Carnarvon who had become acquainted with Carter chose him and a 14 year association began between the two (1908-1922). This cooperation led to the greatest discovery ever in the history of Egypt.

Carnarvon proposed to give Carter a large sum of money to undertake the excavations at Draa Abu el-Naga, the amount was 200 pounds per month. Carter was very excited to be able to do further research in the Theban necropolis, and so he went to work for Carnarvon with the blessing of Gaston Maspero. Carnarvon himself supervised the work of his employees and Weigall the inspector of Upper Egypt, who had difficulty supporting people like Carnarvon, gave him little help in choosing the excavation sites. He believed that people with fortunes were not necessarily good excavators.

Over the next six years, Carter worked to the east of the temple of Deir el-Bahari, he performed strictly controlled research on a wide scale. In 1912 Carter spent a season excavating in the central Delta, but none of these excavations were rich in discoveries. A book dating to the same year was released the same day that the discoveries of Carter and Carnarvon were published. In 1913, Carter began digging in search of the tomb of Amenhotep I, it was discovered in a very poor state of conservation.

And as his excavations had not yielded results in recent years, Theodore Davis aged 77, relinquished his excavation licence in the Valley of the Kings. The repetitiveness of the objects discovered on the site, pushed Carnarvon to try and change the place of excavation, but Carter was focussed on the Valley of the Kings.

In 1915 Carter worked for a month in the tomb of Amenhotep III, which was not in the Valley of the Kings, but in a side valley and discovered a few foundation deposits. However in December 1917 he began his first excavation in the valley between the tombs of Ramses II and Ramses VI oriented northwest - southeast, opposite the entrance to tomb no. 55, which contained objects from the Amarna period. And in a triangular area located below the tomb of Ramses VI, he discovered the remains of structures of stone huts of the workers, who had taken part in the construction of the young pharaoh's tomb.

Excavation work then stopped for various reasons, Lord Carnarvon's illness, the First World War had not yet ended and the departure of Carter for Britain, which was his first visit for three years. In 1920 Carter resumed his search in the Valley of the Kings, this time he concentrated on the valley's entrance for ten weeks. Mountains of rubble were accumulated then carefully examined, the inspection uncovered foundation deposits, ostraca and fragments dating from the reign of Ramses IV.

Excavation stopped again but this time because of the health problems of Carter himself. He travelled back to England and spent six weeks in hospital and another six in convalescence, before returning to Egypt on January 25 1922.

Up to this point all the important discoveries in the Valley of the Kings had been made by Theodore Davies, and before the clearing of the young pharaoh's tomb, a blue faience cup with the name of Tutankhamun had been discovered during the excavation season of 1905 - 1906. In December 1907 a shaft was discovered beneath the tomb of Seti I, which contained pottery, necklaces of flowers and fragments of fabric. Some of them were interesting with beautiful forms but Davies had no interest in them and the whole lot was taken to the Metropolitan Museum. Following a study of the objects in New York it was proved that it was a waste deposit from the funeral ceremonies performed at Tutankhamun's death, as his name was on a large number of the objects. The package was placed at a distance from the tomb to avoid the risk of contamination. This group of objects and cachette proved the existence of Tutankhamun's tomb in the Valley of the Kings.

On February 8, 1922, Carter's excavations began again, the search this time focussing on the east side of the hill housing the tomb of Siptah. This place already excavated by Davis in 1905 was largely covered by accumulations of rubble from the unearthing of Siptah's tomb. According to Carter, these accumulations required ten days, 40 men and 20 helpers to remove them.

In spite of the fact that these excavations were disappointing and again not encouraging, Carter did not want to stop before they had made sure that there was nothing beneath the workers' huts, and tried to reduce expenditure as much as possible. Carter spent five pounds per day for this season of excavations in Thebes, as the material was in place, he then went to England for the summer.

On 11 October Carter returned to Egypt after his trip to England and started work on 1 November 1922 removing the debris in the workers' huts. A step appeared and the workers began to uncover a staircase from this first step leading to a tomb, Carter by now very excited ordered that the work continue all day. At dusk, the 16 steps of the staircase having been cleared one by one, led to a door sealed with plastered stones. The seals of this door bore the representation of the god Anubis dominating the nine enemies of Egypt, but Carter was unable to decipher the texts engraved next to the god.

Despite his enthusiasm and the feeling that he had been rewarded for his work, Carter had the fortitude to shut the site for three weeks and leaving the West Bank, crossed the Nile to the East Bank to send a telegram to Carnarvon, asking him to come to Egypt as quickly as possible. While awaiting Carnavon's arrival from England, Carter prepared everything to recommence the excavation work without wasting time.

On Nov. 23, Lord Carnarvon accompanied by his daughter Eveline Herbert arrived in Luxor. On the afternoon of November 24, work began, an electric light was installed, the entrance and stairs were cleared, these led to a door whose lower part was occupied by the name of Tutankhamun. The next day, the already photographed sealed door, was removed and replaced with a wooden grating. This door led to a sloping corridor, which was completely blocked. This rubble was also removed and the remnants of ancient objects engraved with royal names appeared. Eight metres down another sealed door was cleared, it was a replica of the first.

The tomb was robbed twice shortly after its closure, the first looters took gold and jewellery with the exception of rings, the jewellery in the Cairo Museum is that of the mummy. After the priests and guards had closed the tomb, Tutankhamun received another visit from thieves in search of valuable oils and unguents. Thereafter the tomb was closed by police in antiquity, who filled the corridor with the debris and left the seals with Tutankhamun's titles and those characteristic of the police with the representation of the god Anubis. The tomb's entrance was hidden for 2,000 years beneath the huts of the workers labouring on the tomb of Ramses VI.

On November 26, the crucial moment had arrived, Carter had opened a small hole in the second door into which he introduced a steel rod, he found only emptiness and obscurity. Candles were lit to determine if there were any toxic gases, the hole was then slightly enlarged and Carter brought the candle to it and began to be able to discern the room's details. At that moment Carnarvon and his daughter asked him: "Do you see something?", he then made his now famous reply: "I see marvels." This response showed Carter's state of mind following the discovery after the years of work, his hands and voice were trembling, the hot air escaping from the tomb made the candle's flame quiver and then foreign forms began to appear.

The state of the tomb showed that it was not intact at the time of its discovery, but the excavators still hoped to find a large number of objects. The chests in the hall and annex had been emptied, then refilled and did not contain any valuable items. Very few chests still bore their seals, most of these were broken and the contents looted and the valuables stolen. Only the burial chamber and the treasury with their contents had escaped the looting, the coffins, sarcophagi, chests, canopic chests and shrines occupied their original positions as on the day of the funeral ceremony.

Although Carter saw what remained in the tomb as mere crumbs, he was very proud of his discovery and it took him ten years to clear the tomb and store and record all of its rooms and objects. And from the very beginning, Carter offered to transport the tomb's contents to the Cairo Museum

At this period some other persons joined Carter to aid him in his work, two archaeologists, Sir Flinders Petrie and Arthur Mace, Harry Burton an archaeologist and photographer seconded from the Metropolitan Museum of Art in New York, and a specialist in chemistry, Alfred Lucas.

The tomb contained shrines, coffins, sarcophagi, ritual beds, canopic jars, wrapping strips around the royal mummy, layers of amulets that surrounded him, protective objects and texts from the Book of the Dead. Among the objects discovered in the tomb were accumulations of items from the royal palace, workshops and those belonging to other kings or queens or other funerary furniture, but the name and titles of Tutankhamun were hastily added, as if there was a wish to get rid of things that were useless or unusable. All of these were thoroughly reviewed, classified and registered in a scientific manner.

Excavations were halted in the Valley of the Kings following the discovery of Tutankhamun's tomb bearing the number 62. This tomb is considered one of the smallest buildings in the royal necropolis, and it is believed it was originally cut for a senior official of the young pharaoh, probably Ay. It was appropriated for the young Tutankhamun due to his untimely death and the lack of an already prepared burial place. The tomb's layout, architecture and decoration are very modest and the number of rooms is not worthy of its sovereign, but the history of its discovery and the richness of its contents, attracts visitors of which there are more than 2,000 per day on average. It is believed that the unfinished tomb no. 23 of King Ay located at the west end of the Valley of the Kings, was probably originally destined to be Tuthankamun's tomb.

With the discovery of Tuthankamun's tomb in 1922 it was hoped to find papyri that could instruct us about the history and reign of the pharaoh. But all that was found was rolled linen. As for the reliefs and scenes of the four shrines, they were scenes and inscriptions to assist the king in his life after death. The famous tomb therefore gave no clarification about obscure points in the history of the young pharaoh.

Right : The ou er gold coffin of the king.

PLAN AND DECORATION OF TUTANKHAMUN'S TOMB NO. 62

The tomb's plan is very simple; it consists of a corridor leading to an antechamber, an annex, a burial chamber, which is the only decorated part of the tomb, and a treasury room.

The tomb's entrance carved into the rock is small and leads to a staircase of 16 steps ending in a sloping corridor, 8.08 m long, descending to a room called the antechamber. This is accessed through a door also carved into the rock, this room is oriented north - south and measures 3.55 m wide, 7.85 m in length and 2.68 m in height. The angles of this room are square and the walls are smooth, but do not bear a layer of plaster to receive decorations.

On the south side of the hall, a door leads to a second chamber measuring 4.35 m long, 2.60 m wide and 2.55 m high, its floor is one metre lower than that of the antechamber. It was called the annex by Carter and was considered a room to contain the king's food, again it is not decorated.

The whole of the northern side of the hall opens into the only decorated room in the tomb, which is the burial chamber. It was separated from the hall by a sealed door that was removed by Carter during the

Above : Overall view of the burial chamber with the sarcaphagus and coffin.

clearing of the tomb to enable the removal of the shrines and the chests containing the viscera. The burial chamber is wider than the antechamber measuring 6.37 m long, 4.02 m wide and 3.63 m high. The floor is also one metre lower than that of the antechamber. The walls of the funerary chamber are covered with a layer of plaster on which are drawn and coloured funerary scenes.

Near the northeast corner, a low rectangular door leads to the fourth and last room called the treasury by Carter, which is not decorated. It is orientated north - south, and measures 4.75 m long, 3.80 m broad and 2.33 meters high. This room contained the king's canopic jars, symbolic boats and other treasures like *ushabtis* and the golden statues of the gods and the king, the treasury was also protected by a sealed door.

The burial chamber, which was filled with the shrines, the stone sarcophagus and the wooden and gold coffins, today holds a quartzite sarcophagus, which contains one of the two wooden coffins decorated with gold and semi-precious stones and coloured glass paste, containing the mummy of the king. The quartzite

Above : Hathor and Anubis receive the king in the netherworld.

sarcophagus is covered by a glass plate so that one can look at the badly embalmed mummy in a poor state of preservation, resting in its coffin. The stone cover of the sarcophagus is on the tomb's floor, it is cut from granite. There was certainly a slab of granite available to replace the quartzite lid broken following an accident.

Decoration on the east wall of the burial chamber of tomb no. 62 shows King Tutankhamun's funeral procession. Twelve men dressed in white with their heads attached by white headbands draw a sledge, they are anonymous but a small text above the representation identifies them as (courtiers of the royal palace that go in procession with Osiris Nebkheperure to the west), the word Osiris here shows that the king is dead.

The sledge is surmounted by the ceremonial boat, at the bow are posed a standard in the shape of a sphinx and a small standing figure of the goddess Nephtys lifting both hands in a sign of protection, at the stern is a miniature figure of the goddess Isis. A chapel decorated with two friezes of *uraei* is placed on top of the boat, each *urœus* is surmounted by a solar disk. Inside the chapel, the king's mummy is laid on a bed.

Above : The First Hour of the Amduat with 12 baboons and the early morning representation of the sun god Ra as a beetle.

The north wall of the funerary chamber is divided into three scenes, that furthest to the east shows King Ay as Tutankhamun's successor in a unique way. He is wearing the *khepresh* crown of war and the panther's skin of a *sem* priest, while performing the opening of the mouth rite of death on Tutankhamun, in this scene in the Osirian mummified form arms crossed over the chest. Between King Ay (living), and King Tutankhamun (dead) is a table topped by ritual instruments and a calf's leg. The titles and names of the two kings are written in the cartouches above the scene.

The centre scene according to the text above it, shows Tutankhamun standing in the attitude of a living king being greeted by the goddess Nut in the underworld. The king is wearing a crown and holding a stick in his right hand and a sceptre and an *ankh* sign in his left. The goddess Nut is wearing a closefitting, white dress tied with a belt, whose two ribbons fall the length of her body.

The third scene which is located on the left, shows King Tutankhamun wearing the royal *nemes* headdress, a *usekh* collar on his chest and a kilt, which is long at the back and short in the front. He is embracing the green-skinned, mummified god Osiris, who is welcoming him to the underworld. The king and the god Osiris have become one and the same person here. Behind the king, a man with a long curved beard is standing and clasping the king's right shoulder with his hand, this is his *ka* or spiritual double known by the emblem he is wearing on his head: two arms upraised, with a bull in the middle, in a square topped by a falcon.

The western wall is covered with pictures from the Amduat (Book of the Afterlife). The upper register shows the solar boat preceded by five deities, in the three lower registers 12 baboons are represented, they indicate the first 12 hours of the night.

A piece of the south wall on which are represented Isis and three minor deities, was removed by Carter and is currently in a store. The remaining part shows King Tutankhamun with the *khat* headdress, sandals on his feet, flanked by two deities: Anubis as a jackal-headed man and the goddess Hathor Imentet.

The forms of the king and gods in the tomb scenes are reminiscent of the tomb art of Aten from the preceding period at Tell el-Amarna. This art was not discarded immediately following the death of Akhenaten, but was transmitted to Thebes and employed during the periods of reign that succeeded it.

Above : The Tutankhamun galleries in the Egyptian Museum in Cairo.

THE PLATES

THE FOUR SHRINES (CHAPEL CHESTS) OF TUTANKHAMUN

The mummy, the main component of the royal tomb was preserved in coffins and sarcophagi to assure the deceased's rebirth. Tutankhamun's tomb has given us the most comprehensive set of coffin equipment in Egypt. His mummy was placed in a solid gold coffin with all his jewellery, amulets and his mask, this in turn was put into two more gilded wooden coffins inlaid with coloured glass paste and semi-precious materials, enclosed in a large stone sarcophagus, contained within four shrines.

When the stone blocks separating the burial chamber from the antechamber were removed, the excavators were struck by the first shrine similar to a gigantic wall decorated with gilded *djed* and *tyt* signs engraved on a ground of blue faience, these are the amulets of Osiris and Isis.

The shrines are four in number, they were stacked one within the other above Tutankhamun's mummy, these were placed in the burial chamber and constituted the final four strata above the mummy of the young pharaoh.

The shrines which could be dismantled were made of wood covered with a sheet of engraved gold leaf. The lower edge of each of these shrines was covered with a sheet of copper. A folding door was arranged in the east side of each, these were closed with ebony bolts and every door was fitted with two additional rings to take the cord of a seal, but the fourth shrine was never sealed.

The dimensions of the shrines were adapted to fit into the small funerary chamber, so they were made after the king's death when it was known where he would be buried. They filled almost all of the funerary chamber's space, which made disassembly and removal of the fifty-one elements particularly difficult; such manual work alone took 24 days. The shrines weighed a total of 500 kilos.

The dimensions of the chamber lead us to believe that the panels were laid against the wall one by one and then erected from the fourth to the first shrine. More than fifteen markers were left by the carpenters to indicate the method of assembly and orientation of the panels.

The third and fourth shrines mimic the external shape of an Archaic period temple of the south, the engraved decoration refers to funeral ceremonies where the spirits of the canopic jars appear.

EXTERNAL SHRINE

Length: 508 cm, width 328 cm, height: 275 cm.

It is made of heavy cedar panels of which both faces have gilded plaster with inlays. The side panels of the shrine are decorated with the fertility amulets of Isis the double *tyt* knot, and hieroglyphics like the *djed* spine of Osiris symbolizing stability, they are set against a background of bright blue faience. Two *wadjet* eyes adorn the north side.

The interior walls of the shrine bear multiple inscriptions whose formulas are derived from the Book of the Dead and the Book of the

Divine Cow (Legend of the destruction of humanity). A hollow moulding on the inside of the shrine's wall represents the cow, and the ceiling is decorated with solar disks and thirteen winged vultures.

Between the first shrine on the exterior and the second was a shroud resting on a wooden support. The burial cloth is dark brown linen, coarsely woven, sewn and decorated with large daisies in gilded bronze, it measures 5.5 m x 4,5 m, supported by a frame consisting of nine pieces of wood plastered, lacquered and gilded. It was a night filled with stars, but torn apart under the weight of the daisies.

SECOND SHRINE

Length: 374 cm, width 235 cm, height: 225 cm.

The shrine has a sloping ceiling which imitates the primitive temple of Upper Egypt know as (*per-er*); its sixteen panels are covered with engraved plaster reliefs composed of images and inscriptions, covered with gold leaf.

The outer surface of the two doors is decorated with a moulding of the king's funeral before the god Osiris on the left and Ra-horakhty on the right. Isis and Nephtys appear on the wall of the chapel, they must lead the mourning for the god king.

The interior is dominated by the sky Nut under the *nub* sign (any) and on the sides of the ceiling, five vultures are represented. On the panel inside the right door is a messenger with the head of an ass and a guardian of the afterlife. The name of Tutankhamun is inscribed here together with the name of the god Aten.

The texts engraved on the inside and outside are from the Pyramids Texts of the Old Kingdom and the Book of the Dead. There are also magical texts engraved in an incomprehensible way, no doubt aimed at routing the enemy forces that the pharaoh was likely to encounter after his death.

THIRD SHRINE

Length: 340 cm, width 192 cm, height: 215 cm.

It resembles the second with the ceiling in the form of (per-er); it is an assemblage of ten panels and on the inner walls are scenes and texts from the Book of the Dead. These represent guardians with the heads of humans, antelope, deer and crocodiles with one or two knives, thus permitting the deceased pharaoh to pass beyond the night to achieve unification with the sun god at dawn.

THE INNER OR FOURTH SHRINE

Length: 290 cm, width 148 cm, height: 190 cm

It has a vaulted ceiling in the style of the temples and palaces of Lower Egypt from the Pre-dynastic period (per-nu). When it was placed in the tomb it completely enclosed the sarcophagus, which must have been trimmed before its insertion.

This shrine consists of five elements with bas-relief representations of the divinities Isis, Nephtys, Serket and Neith, Anubis, the dogs of Anubis, the four sons of Horus, Amsety, Duamutef, Hapy and Kebehsenuef, and the gods Hapi and Thoth in two forms, supporting the sky, and finally Horus.

The main text is taken from the Book of the Dead, Chapter XVII, which is a long composition about the sun god Ra and the doctrinal theory, with many comments on the god and the deceased. The ceiling shows the goddess Nut in the form of a winged woman spreading her wings.

THE SARCOPHAGUS AND COFFINS OF TUTANKHAMUN

The tomb of King Tutankhamun provides the most comprehensive set of protective measures ever brought to light. The mummy was placed in three coffins, two of gilded wood and one of solid gold, enclosed in a huge stone sarcophagus, which was itself contained within four shrines, whose dimensions were adapted to fit into the small funerary chamber.

The kings and queens of the New Kingdom were buried in a series of coffins and enclosed in a sarcophagus. The coffins were generally mummiform in gilded wood or cartonnage, some are in stone but sometimes a king has a gold coffin, like the young Pharaoh Tutankhamun.

There is nothing comparable to what awaited the spectators in the burial chamber of the tomb of Tutankhamun, the royal mummy was enclosed in a series of coffins and sarcophagi, themselves surrounded by shrines.

THE GRANITE SARCOPHAGUS

This sarcophagus is from a single block of quartzite and it rested on the corners of four calcite blocks. Its cover is carved from a block of red granite painted yellow to match the casing. The lid was cracked in the centre due to an accident during its hasty installation, this break was plugged with plaster. The box's decoration is formed of the four goddesses Isis, Nephtys, Serket and Neith sculpted in high relief at the four corners. The deities are spreading their wings in the act of protection, they meet on the short sides of the sarcophagus and almost touch on the longer sides.

Each goddess is wearing her emblem on her head, Isis a throne that symbolizes the legitimacy of the throne, Nephtys a house, which symbolizes royalty, Neith has two crossed bows symbolizing war and protection, and Selket, a scorpion symbolizing the healing of diseases and health. The lower part of the sarcophagus shows a repetitive pattern of the double *djed* and *tyt* amulets.

This sarcophagus is currently in the tomb containing the first and largest of the coffins and inside is the pharaoh's mummy, now in a poor condition.

When the broken lid of the sarcophagus was lifted, a layer of cloth was discovered, it hid beneath is the three coffins of the young pharaoh, of which the two larger ones were of gilded wood with inlays and the smaller one was of solid gold.

THE FIRST COFFIN

Of gilded wood with inlays (see picture page 25) it now rests in the tomb of Tutankhamun in the Valley of the Kings, and contains the royal remains. The coffin is magnificent, its decoration in high relief is the figure of Osiris or even that of the mummified king. The king is wearing the *khat* headdress surmounting his hair and the vulture Nekhbet and cobra Wadjet on his forehead. He has a lovely face, young and smiling, a long braided beard, arms crossed over the chest with the symbols of royalty, two sceptres, and some bracelets around his wrists and a large necklace around his neck.

All along the body, the two winged goddesses Isis and Nephtys are standing dressed in long, closefitting robes and wearing a necklace, spreading their large wings around the king's body, and raising their arms to the level of the king's shoulders. Two vertical lines of hieroglyphs descend vertically towards the king's feet, the rest of the body is covered with incisions in the form of fish scales. The goddess Isis is represented winged, kneeling on the *nub* sign of gold at the king's feet, she is wearing her symbol (throne) on the head and raises her arms and wings in a protecting action.

THE MIDDLE COFFIN

Length: 204 cm, maximum height: 78 cm, width: 68 cm.

When Carter lifted the lid of the first coffin, he did not expect to find a second coffin wrapped in a shroud made of wool and decorated with garlands of olive leaves, lotus petals and cornflowers attached to small pieces of papyrus.

After being cleaned the coffin appeared in all its splendour, it is of wood covered with a sheet of gold leaf and decorated with a cloisonné pattern of inlays of coloured glass paste and semiprecious stones, surrounded by thin strips of welded gold. The lid is equipped with four silver handles, two on each side for ease of carrying.

The figure of the god Osiris or the mummified king is portrayed on the lid. He is wearing the striped *nemes* headdress with the two deities Nekhbet and Wadjet on his forehead, the lobes of the ears that appear below the *nemes*, are pierced. His face is beautiful and the features are well drawn, they have a calm and serious expression; it is believed that this coffin was not originally intended for the young pharaoh. The obsidian eyes are outlined by a line of blue glass paste; the eyebrows are semi-circular and parallel to the blue lines of the eyes. The nose is straight and the mouth is full, the king's beard is braided with golden wire, it is false and curves upwards. The king is wearing a wide neck collar.

The two arms are crossed on his chest and both hands covered with gold leaf are holding two sceptres, the *heka* and *nekhekh*. Below the hands folded on his chest, the winged Wadjet cobra and Nekhbet vulture are spreading their wings around the king to protect him. They are holding the *shen* ring in cornelian encircled with turquoise, which symbolizes eternity.

The main decorative pattern of the coffin is the feather that covers the upper third of the lid and body, and even the bodies of the two winged deities on the upper part of the lid. But all of the lower part from the navel to the fan-shaped feet is covered with another motif of fish scales, except for the two vertical lines of hieroglyphs running around the coffin. At the back, the goddess Isis is represented winged and kneeling on the *nub* sign of gold, spreading her wings to protect the deceased.

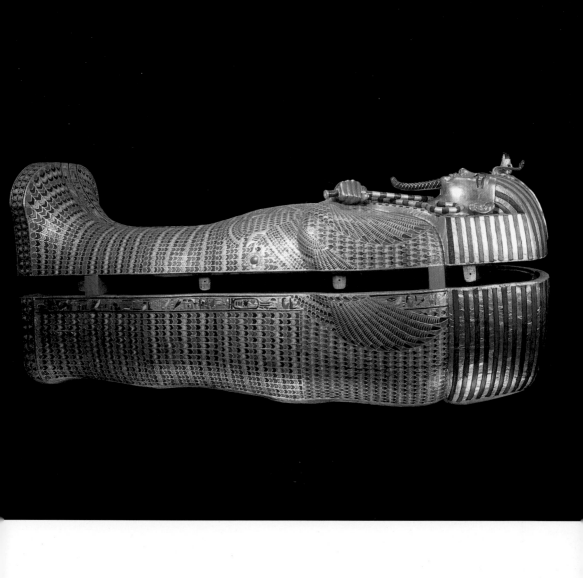

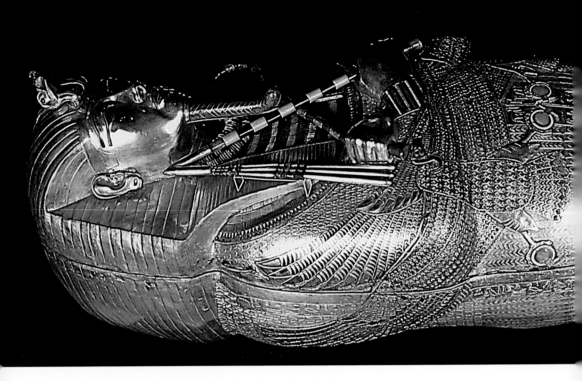

THE INNER COFFIN

Length: 187 cm, height: 51 cm, width: 51, 3 cm, weight: 110.4 kg of 22 carat gold

The coffin is made of gold and is the largest item ever made of solid gold, it was beaten and chased both on the inside and the outside. Its 110 kilos make the coffin the most impressive ever uncovered. Apart from the value of the material used, it was also an artistic masterpiece, especially the face that bears the traits of the sovereign Tutankhamun as young, handsome and dreamy.

he gilded coffin shows the king with the royal headdress or striped *nemes*, the two goddesses, the *urœus* (Wadjet) and the vulture (Nekhbet), are placed on the forehead. Beneath the chin the long, divine curved beard of gold is inlaid with lapis-blue glass paste; it is braided with golden wire. The eyelids and lines of makeup are of blue glass paste.

This coffin is in the form of a mummiform Osiris holding in his hands crossed on the chest, the *heka* sceptre and the *nekhekh* flail, symbols of royalty. On the crossed wrists there are wide bracelets inlaid with stones.

Around his neck, he is wearing a necklace composed of a double row of lozenges or disks of gold, coloured glass paste and faience. On his chest is an impressive *usekh* necklace richly decorated with stones and consisting of 11 rows of coloured glass paste beads, broken in the middle by a rectangle of several rows of coloured beads.

And despite the fact that the coffin has handles, it was difficult to separate the lid from the case as there were ten silver nails with gold heads in addition to the large amounts of resin, which had been poured onto the lid and inside the other two coffins. This resin filled the space between the two coffins completely and had the effect on setting of sticking the inner coffin to the middle one.

Separating the lid was very difficult and took a lot of time using a high heat while protecting the inside with zinc plates. Once removed, the inside of the coffin was subjected to more heat and solvents to remove the substance. The heated bitumen damaged the inlays and decorative elements and calcite inlays that formed the eyes.

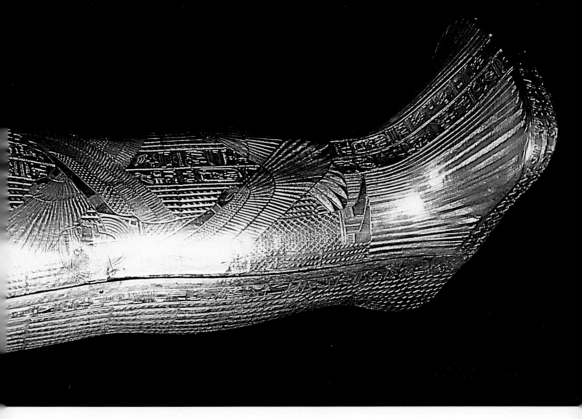

On the chest, two winged goddesses who are the protective divinities of Upper and Lower Egypt, Nekhbet the vulture and Wadjet the cobra are represented. Their bodies are completely inlaid with coloured glass paste and semi-precious stones, and they are holding in their claws the *shen* ring inlaid with cornelian, they cover the king's chest to the shoulders with their interlaced wings.

A long strip of hieroglyphic text traverses the body of the coffin vertically from the naval to the feet. Further down at thigh level, the two protective winged goddess guardians of the dead and mourners, Isis and Nephtys cross their wings to protect the king's body, they are engraved and incised in the coffin without any inlays. The words they recite for this purpose are included in the double middle band of hieroglyphs, another short inscription runs around the coffin.

A representation of Isis with large spread wings fills all the available space under the king's feet. She is kneeling on the sign symbolizing gold and lifting her arms and is described as (The all-embracing Isis, mother of the God). On her head is a smooth tripartite wig attached by a ribbon on the forehead, she is wearing jewellery, bracelets around the wrists and forearms, and a necklace around his neck. Her closefitting dress with a pattern of fish scales and two shoulder straps ends at the feet.

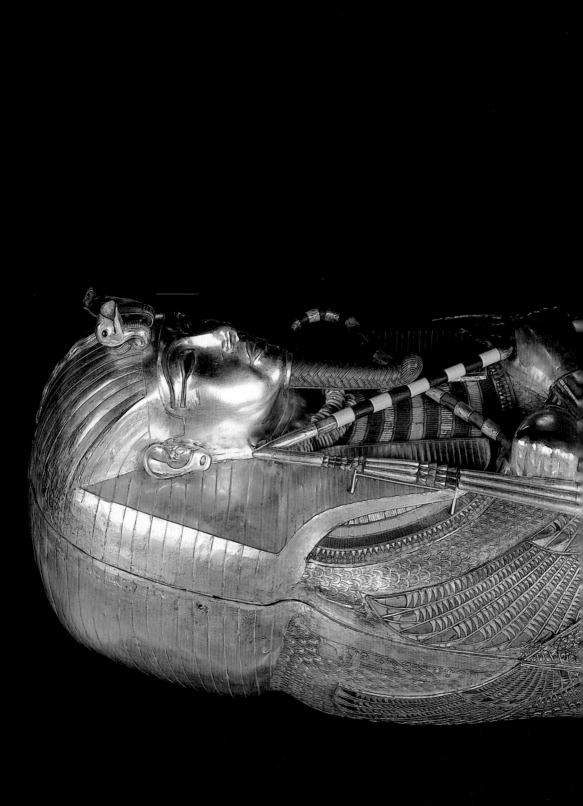

MASK OF TUTANKHAMUN

Height: 54 cm, weight: 11 kg.

The is the most famous piece from the funerary collection of Tutankhamun, a marvellous life-size mask of excellent workmanship. It is a masterly portrait and testimony to the excellence of the art of the Egyptian goldsmiths. It was placed on the face of the mummy to protect it and its removal was not easy because the unguents, which covered the mummy had turned black over the years and acted like an adhesive.

Carter had decided to examine the mummy, to take off the strips and to remove the jewellery and amulets, and when he was able to observe the mask he found that it was worked in a superb fashion using two sheets of beaten gold and assembled by hammering, the surface was decorated, polished and incrusted with multi-coloured high quality stones and glass paste. It remains unequalled among the *chefs d'œuvre* of Egyptian goldsmiths.

The pharaoh has the royal headdress, which is the *nemes* headscarf knotted at the back, which covers the king's head completely and extends over his back. From the front, the two rounded ends of the *nemes* cover the chest; their stripes are of blue glass paste. On the forehead the two protective goddesses, the Nekhbet vulture and the Wadjet snake worked in solid gold and decorated with semi-precious stones and coloured glass paste, rise up.

The eyes of black obsidian and white quartz provided with reddish spots to give the impression of liveliness are very realistic; the outline and eyebrows are inlaid with lapis lazuli and the eyebrows end on the same level as the black line applied to the eyes. The nose is slightly turned up with a rounded tip; the lower part of the face is somewhat elongated, the fleshy mouth is nicely drawn. In each ear lobe is a hole for the wearing of a jewel. The beard is braided and curled back and it is decorated with glass paste set in gold partitions.

Around the neck and on the chest is a broad collar formed of twelve rows of beads made of glass paste inlays, turquoise, lapis lazuli and quartz; the collar is linked to each shoulder by a falcon's head decorated with obsidian.

The inscription engraved in ten lines of hieroglyphics starting on the right shoulder and ending on the left, represents an additional protection formula. In this inscription, the various parts of the body were identified with the body parts corresponding to the divinities: (your face is Anubis, your right eye is the night boat, your left eye is the diurnal boat, your eyebrows correspond to the companion of the nine gods). This inscription was introduced during the New Kingdom in Chapter 151 of the Book of the Dead.

MUMMIFICATION

Mummification in Egypt was not always of an equal quality and underwent multiple variations depending on the era. It went through a trial period up to the 18th Dynasty, success in the 19th, then a swift decline at the beginning of the Persian invasion. Behind mummification is the idea of immortalising the human body to enable the soul's survival.

The order of operations is as follows: Removal of the brain, evisceration, a first body wash, processing of viscera, dehydration of the body, a second washing, stuffing of the cranium and cavities, special treatment for the nails, eyes and external genital organs, anointing and body massage after dehydration, the final preparations before covering with bandages, treatment of the body with resin and finally the wrapping in bandages.

The first step was to remove the brain that was just a banal internal organ to the Egyptians. It was most often extracted through the nasal passage using long curved or spiral bronze hooks, the entry of the bronze rod sometimes caused the nasal passage to collapse with the action of coming and going. The brain was extracted in fragments, sometimes it was removed by passing it through the spongy turbinate nose bones,

With the brain removed, the embalmers tackled the viscera, using a piece of prepared flint the embalmer made a vertical incision of about ten centimetres in the left side. Through this gaping wound, the main specialist would draw out the intestines, stomach, liver, spleen, and kidneys. The embalmer up to his armpits in the entrails used his hands to extract the lungs in a final stage.

The heart was the object of special care and was left in its usual place after mummification, as it was the seat of emotional, intellectual and physical life. When the deceased was brought before the court in the afterlife, his heart was weighed on the great scales of truth. Isolated from the man, the heart could not lie, it was essential during the trial, then in the eternal life.

The body was subjected to a washing ritual using water or palm wine to rid the skin of any waste, not only was the outer surface cleaned but also the insides received the same treatment.

The organs that were removed from the body were treated separately, the embalmer washed and then placed them in natron as with the body, then coated them with hot gum resin and delicately swaddled them in several metres of cloth strips. The embalmer used four packages. which he placed in four funerary urns.

The jars in which the viscera were gathered were given the name canopic vases by archaeologists. Canopus was a port located at one of the mouths of the Nile on the site of present day Abukir. In the Greek period the form of Osiris worshipped in Canopus was a pitcher closed with a top in the shape of the head of Osiris, from which comes the use of the word Canopus for jars with stoppers that represent heads.

These vases were manufactured in baked clay for the more humble, in calcite, hard stone or alabaster for the richer. Four in number, they were surmounted by the heads of the four sons of Horus, spirit protectors of the entrails. The intestines are folded up in the vase with the head of the monkey god Hapy, the liver rolled into a tube is in the canopic vase with the falcon-headed Kebehsnuef, the stomach was destined for the vase with the human-headed Amsety, as for the lungs, they were under the protection of the jackal-headed Duamutef.

After the lid was sealed with plaster, these canopic vases accompanied the deceased. They were often assembled in a chest divided into four compartments, at the side of the sarcophagus.

Above : The Tutankhamun galleries in the Egyptian Museum in Cairo.

CANOPIC CHEST

Overall height: 85.5 cm, width of each side of the base: 54 cm

The viscera of Tutankhamun were introduced into four miniature gilded wooden sarcophagi inlaid with coloured glass, placed in four canopic jars and locked in a calcite chest. A wooden shrine surrounded the chest containing the calcite canopic vases, which was itself protected by an open canopy decorated with an elaborate frieze. The whole ensemble was under the protection of the goddesses Isis, Nephtys, Serket and Neith. The shrine with all its contents was put into the treasury behind the god Anubis.

This chest when found was covered, as were a large number of chests and statues, in linen fabric, then placed in a large wooden shrine, whose dimensions did not permit it to be put into the tomb without being dismantled. The workers left a large number of benchmarks to facilitate the reassembly of the panels in the young pharaoh's tomb.

During the 18th Dynasty, most of the viscera coffers contained four compartments to hold vases with human-headed shaped stoppers. This head is the portrait of King Tutankhamun represented with the *nemes* from which rise up the *uræus* and the vulture.

The chest is made from a block of semi-translucent calcite and placed on a second plastered and gilded sledge, whose lower dado is decorated with the *djed* and *tyt* signs associated with Osiris and Isis. The north and south sides are equipped with four big bronze hooks that serve as handles.

The chest's pitched lid mimics the appearance of a sanctuary, it is slanting and connected to the body of the chest by ropes passed through rings and sealed. The decoration at the front is of a kneeling divinity, probably the winged goddess of justice Maat, a ribbon is attached to her hair and she is wearing a long, closefitting dress.

At the four corners of the piece of furniture are carvings in high relief, of the four protective goddesses: Isis, Nephtys, Serket and Neith. Each goddess has long slender limbs and is wearing a long, tight dress with shoulder straps and is looking at the goddess on her left. On her head is her emblem; a throne for Isis, a house for Nephtys, a scorpion for Serket and crossed bows for Neith.

The inscriptions engraved on the side of the chest invoking the protection of the four deities and relating to the spirits, are coloured blue contrasting strongly with the wax colour of the calcite.

In each vase is a sarcophagus of beaten gold wrapped in linen decorated with feathers to contain the king's viscera, protected by the four sons of Horus. They are: Duamutef the stomach, Amsety the liver, Kebehsnuef the stomach and Hapi the lungs. The heart was removed from the body at the time of mummification, mummified on its own, and then returned to the body and covered with a scarab.

The four identical heads of the young pharaoh in calcite evoke life reborn. The king is wearing the striped *nemes*, his eyes are made up and the eyebrows are well drawn, the pupil is painted black and the inner and outer corners of the eyes have a light touch of red. The holes in the ears and the folds in the neck were made using a black filament. The details of the two royal animals Nekhbet and Wadjet posed at the top of the *nemes* are painted black, the lips are coloured red.

GILDED WOODEN NAOS OF THE CANOPIC VASES

Height: 198 cm, length: 153 cm, width 122 cm.

The sarcophagus, caskets and shrines of decreasing size were placed one inside the other. This idea was reused in a more simple fashion for the conservation of the body's viscera.

A wooden gold plated *naos*, which rose majestically on a sledge to facilitate its movement, contained a canopic chest. On lifting the calcite lid, four royal heads appeared, they were used as stoppers for the four vases placed in the four compartments cut in the calcite, including coffins containing the king's mummified viscera.

The wooden shrine comprises four corner posts, which bear the complete titulary of Tutankhamun and supports a large cornice crowned with a frieze of *uræi* inlaid with coloured glass paste and faience, surmounted by solar disks inlaid with turquoise, red and green coloured glass paste.

Four figurines of deities are placed, one on each side of the chest, they are nicely worked following the style of the art of the Aten period wearing beautiful transparent dresses. They look towards the chest having the responsibility of protecting the canopic jars with their open arms. These goddesses are Isis, recognizable by the throne she is wearing on her head, Nephtys by a basket in an enclosure, Serket denoted by a scorpion and Neith goddess of war and Sais, carrying her shield.

These goddesses are among the most beautiful carvings bequeathed to us by pharaonic Egypt. Their bodies are slender and slightly elongated and they are wearing a pleated, skin-tight tunic with short sleeves and a veil on the head, their hair falling freely at the back is held in place by a tie at the neck. The head is slightly turned to one side in a delicate movement. The eyes and eyebrows are well drawn emphasized by a black line.

The dado is also surmounted by a ledge and a frieze of *uræi*. Each of its gilded inner walls is decorated with bas reliefs representing each of the four goddesses facing one of the four spirit gods, guardians of the viscera, these are Amsety, Hapi, Duamutef and Kebehsnuef.

USHABTIS

Ushabtis are statuettes or small funerary figurines bearing features identical to those of the deceased, which accompany him in his tomb .

They are called ushabtis or shabtis. Ushabti is a name which derives from the word ushab meaning "to answer or reply"; they are thus the servers, who answer the call of the gods to carry out agricultural work in the fields of Iaru or paradise. The name shabti derives from the word shawab, which means "wood" (of the persea tree), the material from which these statuettes were manufactured during the Middle Kingdom.

In ancient Egypt those who had the means were accustomed to placing statues of servants in their tombs to serve and assist them in the afterlife, and to carry out manual tasks. During the Old Kingdom, the king and his close relatives were to meet in the fields of Iaru in the afterlife, the agricultural fields of Osiris, into which the deceased were permitted in the role of workers as they were into the earthly fields of the pharaoh. They should cultivate the soil to the profit of the master and also themselves, in order to ensure both the king's prosperity and their own eternal survival at the same time.

The ushabtis themselves were to plough these fields, sow them and harvest them to ensure their own continued existence; therefore the king had the possibility of making his subjects work for him. A great number of statues have been brought to light representing the people, who carried out various kinds of tasks: brewing beer, making bread dough, putting the bread in the oven, manufacturing pottery, plucking geese and carrying sandals, etc.

It was during the Middle Kingdom that the first examples of ushabtis appeared, limited to one statue per tomb. Their role was above all to answer in place of the deceased, when he was called upon to take part in certain material labour during his stay in the netherworld: the cultivation and irrigation of the paradisiacal fields, and the movement of sand from the East to the West. The ushabti was also responsible for carrying out all humble tasks in the place of the deceased and especially agricultural labour, relieving him from national drudgery, helped by magic spells, as we learn from Formula III in Chapter 7 of the Book of the Dead. Tombs at the end of the Middle Kingdom only contained one ushabti, a substitute for the deceased.

During the New Kingdom, many tombs were furnished with ushabtis in various materials. The rich accumulated a considerable number, which could reach 700, covering the year, week, month and season and feast days as well. Those of the nobles carried their tools in their hands: hoes, pickaxes, baskets, picks, according to their specialization, and sacks on their backs. As for the king, his two hands holding the badges of power were folded on his chest, and at his side it was the custom to place miniature implements.

At the time of Tutankhamun, the royal burials were furnished with two *ushabtis;* however, 413 were found in the tomb of Tutankhamun. The 365 *ushabtis* were divided in the following manner: a statue for each day of the year intended to carry out daily tasks, and these statues were divided into teams of ten supervised by 36 foremen and 12 superintendents. The *ushabtis* were placed in painted black boxes, 11 in the treasury (176 statues), 14 in the appendix (236 statues) and a final one, which had been moved from the annex to the antechamber.

The statuettes found in the tomb of Tutankhamun depict the king as the mummified Osiris, however the materials, sizes and inscriptions are very diverse: the facial features are very clear and well drawn, the eyebrows are lengthened, the eyes are wide open and the small mouth is smiling. The king wears the Osirian coat, a false beard and a collar around the neck. His arms are crossed on his chest and his titulary is engraved on the body of each statuette.

Some *ushabtis* are of wood with traces of black paint and gold leaf, while others are completely gilded. Many examples are of faience or carved from calcite, granite, limestone and sandstone blocks. As for the hairstyles, crowns and wigs, they are diverse; there is the *nemes* (royal headscarf), the *khat,* the principal crowns and wigs like the fizzy Nubian style, one with layers of curls and the smooth tripartite wig with the frontal *uræus* to which the vulture is sometimes added.

Some ush ibtis hold the royal insignias in the hands crossed over the chest and conversely, a great number of hoes, metal pickaxe parts, faience and wood were found in the treasury and the annex.

USHABTI WITH WHITE CROWN

Height: 63 cm.

An ushabti found in one of the chests in the treasury, it represents the king in royal stance with the White Crown *(desheret)* as sovereign of Lower Egypt. The statue is almost completely gilded except for the face and hands, which are left in the natural wood.

The White Crown still retains its gilding and is in a good state of preservation. A protective bronze uræus rests on the forehead. The face of the statue is beautiful and bears some traces of the art of the Aten period: almond eyes made up with a black line, moderately open and surmounted by long well drawn eyebrows. The nose is long and the red painted smiling mouth is a little broad, the ears are large with the bored lobes showing traces of earrings.

The body of the statuette is mummified, the arms crossed on the chest with the royal insignias: the gilded bronze *heka* and *nekhekh* remain in place, while the *nekhekh* flail has a sheet of fine gold leaf, which still covers it. A text of two vertical lines of hieroglyphics is engraved all along the body.

USHABTI WITH WHITE CROWN

Height: 61,5 cm.

A mummiform *ushabti* wearing the White Crown of Upper Egypt *(hedjet)*; it was found in the same chest as that containing the *ushabti* with White Crown in the treasury.

The statuette with beautiful and expressive facial features represents King Tutankhamun in Osirian attitude. The wide open eyes highlighted by a black line are surmounted by long raised eyebrows; the nose is small and straight, the small, slightly smiling mouth is well drawn, the chin is short, the neck is shortened and the ears are large. Around the neck a broad necklace covers the shoulders and part of the chest.

The king is wearing an elongated White Crown; on the forehead is an *uræus* to which is added the head of a bronze vulture. The whole of the figurine is gilded except for the face and hands, which are in the natural wood. The hands are crossed over the chest; they still retain one of the two royal insignia, which is the crook or the *heka*. Four lines of hieroglyphic text are engraved on the body of the *ushabti*.

USHABTI WITH NUBIAN WIG

Height: 54 cm

A simple and beautiful ushabti superbly carved in wood left in its natural colour; as usual it represents the mummified king, the two arms crossed on the chest, but the royal insignias are missing although the grooves in the hands are quite distinct.

The jewellery of the statue comprises a fine headband around the forehead, a *usekh* collar covering the shoulders and most of the chest and a bracelet, all of gold.

The statuette is wearing a Nubian wig, which was a type of wig worn by women as well as men. Tutankhamun is wearing this wig on several chests, in gilded wooden chapels and in the scenes of everyday life, especially those of hunting in the marshes. A collection of vases was found in tomb No 55 in the Valley of the Kings with stoppers in the form of heads wearing this kind of wig.

On the forehead of the *ushabti* are attached two protective elements, which are the vulture, Nekhbet and the cobra, Wadjet. The eyes are large and open, the nose is small and the thin lipped mouth gives the impression of a mocking smile.

A large text of four columns in white from Chapter 6 of the Book of Dead covers an extensive part of the figure's body.

USHABTI PRESENTED BY NAKHTMIN

Height: 52 cm

The general and royal scribe Nakhtmin presented five examples of ushabtis in the tomb of King Tutankhamun as a mark of his devotion to his master, at the court during his terrestrial life and in the afterlife.

This very delicately carved wooden ushabti is one of the five offered by Nakhtmin; it represents Tutankhamun wearing the royal nemes headscarf decorated with black stripes. The eyes, eyebrows, lips and features of the collar also bear traces of black.

The gilding is still clear on the frontal uræus, the fine band around the forehead and the flail. The facial features are beautiful, the eyes are wide open; the ears are large with bored lobes, both of the long ends of the nemes fall to the right and left of the neck so hiding part of the collar.

The arms crossed over the chest are holding the two royal insignias, the nekhekh flail and the heka crook of gilded bronze, but these have lost their gilding today. The two arms are surmounted by the representation of a ba-bird, whose spread wings represent the soul of the deceased. The bird's head appears between the king's two crossed hands and its wings cover part of the royal figure's arms up to the shoulders. The body is covered with six columns of hieroglyphics.

USHABTI OF TUTANKHAMUN WITH THE CROWN OF WAR

Height: 48 cm.

It is a sculpture of a very high quality carved in wood without any decoration except for some details of the king's body, the usekh collar around the neck, the flail, which is one of the sceptres that Tutankhamun holds in his hand, the frontal uræus and the headband on the forehead are covered with very fine gold leaf.

This figure is a mummy wearing the blue (khepresh) crown of war. The face is carved in a fine and elegant style, the eyes and the eyebrows are drawn with a dark black line.

A double column of hieroglyphics giving us the formula of the ushabtis, covers the middle part of the figurine.

RECUMBENT STATUETTE OF TUTANKHAMUN

Length of statue: 42,2 cm, width: 12 cm. Height of coffin 4,3 cm.

This statue carved from a single piece of cedar wood and wrapped in strips like a mummy, was found in the treasury inside a small box painted black and shaped like an Osirian cenotaph with a curved roof.

It represents the image of the royal mummy lying on a low bier or bed adorned with elongated lions, whose heads rise above that of the king; the bed's legs and feet take the form of lion's legs.

According to an inscription engraved between the legs of the lions under the two lateral sides of the framework of the bed, it was a shrine dedicated to Nebkheperure from Maia: "The servant useful to his Master, who carries out the perfect things for his Master in the splendid place, the chief of work in the place of eternity on the Western Bank, that its Master likes, the royal scribe, governor of works in the necropolis, steward of the treasure".

touches of gilding and black paint. The eyebrows, eyes and mouth are painted black and white. The king is wrapped in his shroud, arms crossed on his chest, wearing a collar made of strands of pearls.

The king's image is accompanied by a bird on each side, both of which are extending a wing across the breast of the deceased as far as the elbow. At the tips of these wings, the handles of the two sceptres, which the king would have held in his hands but which have disappeared, would have passed; they were probably manufactured from a precious substance.

The birds are different: on the left, is the *ba*-bird with a human head, as for that on the right, it has the head of a falcon. On the median and transverse bands of text, the inscriptions bear the names of Hapy, (one of the four sons of Horus) and Anubis. On the left side, two others evoke the favours of Kebehsenuef (a son of Horus) and Osiris, and on the right, Amsety (a son of Horus), Anubis, Duamutef (a son of Horus), and the name of Horus.

This bed was significant in several ways due to its connection with female sexuality; it was regarded as a nuptial bed and not as a simple piece of funerary furniture, the deceased would be regenerated while being united with his wife. The bed thus materializes this mystical marriage and this idea reminds us of Osiris' return to life, when he found his virility through Isis.

The *ba* (the spirit) and Horus are present on the bed. The deceased is promised that he will join with the cosmic forces and undergo a sort of confrontation between the individual and his own consciousness. The material part of man lies in two entities, the *ka* (double) and *ba* (the spirit). Indeed, the *ka* is a vital element of a human being, which is separate from the body while the *ba* is a variable component, a human-headed bird that enables the deceased to move physically. The *ba* dwells in the mummy or any image of death, it is thanks to it that human beings can come into contact with the world of the invisible; it is destined to remain in the sky while the body is in the *douat* or the underworld.

The bird on the left of the recumbent figure represents the spirit that departs from the deceased and returns to find it again; it is Osiris, the aspect of what was (yesterday); on the statue, the legend of Chapter 85 from the Book of the Dead speaks of the transformation of the deceased into the *ba* of Ra, among its metamorphoses in the netherworld. As for the bird on the right, it is the falcon that precedes the new appearance of the soul, which having successfully undergone the rites, is born again. It is thus Horus, destined to ascend to the throne of his father, the renewed manifestation of the dead which will exist (tomorrow). The king will thus undergo the tests between the poles of yesterday and tomorrow, the west and the east, which concept is evoked by the two lions with their heads framing that of the king. The two lions are Aker, who personify the earth and receiving the dead.

Ultimately, our symbol of death guarantees the presence of all the elements essential to achieve the deceased's rebirth in the future life, which are: the presence of the names of the divinities (the four sons of Horus), who protect the vital organs of the body. The band of text, which runs vertically along the body of the statue to the feet, is an invocation addressed to the goddess Nut: "O my Nut mother extend over me, make me blend with the imperishable stars which are in you". The mummy of the king between the two poles of yesterday and tomorrow, expresses the present. Female sexuality is represented by the bed and confers an important role on the wife in the life of the deceased, which was essential to his survival in the netherworld.

STATUES OF DIVINITIES

The discovery of Tutankhamun's tomb brought to light 35 statues in twenty two black painted *naosoi* (chests) with double sealed doors, which were found in the treasury. Among these figures were those representing the king and others anthropomorphic divinities like the four sons of Horus, the two mourners Isis and Nephtys, cosmic gods like Ptah, Atum, the goddess Menkaret, who carries the king on her head and two black painted figurines of the god Ihy, each of them holding a sistrum.

Statues of the gods have a value in that they commemorate the myths and beliefs of the ancient Egyptians, the ritual and customs associated with death. They served good or evil or had magic powers.

STATUE OF THE GOD ATUM

Height: 63 cm

One of the 35 statues belonging to Tutankhamun found in the black painted wooden chests in the treasury, inside his tomb.

Atum is one of the most important gods of the Egyptian pantheon, his name means (The Perfect One), (The Complete One), (That which cannot be defined). He sometimes takes a human form with the head of a ram or a cat, wearing the double crown and holding the *ankh* and the *was*. This god does not have a companion or wife; Shu and Tefnut are his children.

Atum presides over the Heliopolis Ennead and was associated with Ra and Khepry, which are the other forms of the sun. His town of origin is Heliopolis or *Oun*, he represents thus the bond between Thebes (southern *Oun*) and Heliopolis (northern *Oun*).

The wooden statue of Atum is completely covered by a sheet of thick gold leaf, except for the eyes, which are well defined with black. The god is represented as a mummy wrapped in a sheath; the two arms are crossed on the chest. He wears a smooth wig with long locks from which appear two large ears; the neck is encircled by a broad *usekh* collar containing several rows, which covers the whole chest and part of the shoulders.

The nose is long and the mouth closed, the gaze of the eyes and features of the face give it a wise and serious impression. The statue is restrained, there are no details to tell us that it is Atum, no crown nor insignias. But an inscription on the base of the statue traced in yellow paint, names it: (Atum, the living god).

STATUE OF THE GODDESS SEKHMET

Height: 55.2 cm

The goddess Sekhmet is one of oldest and most important divinities of the Egyptian pantheon; she belongs to the group of lioness goddesses made up of Wadjet, Pakhet, Bastet, Hathor and Mut. Her name means (The Powerful One) and she represents the manifestation of the eye of the god Ra.

She is generally represented as a lioness or a woman with a lioness's head, clothed in the close fitting dress with two straps of the goddesses. Her cult was attested to in Memphis from the Old Kingdom, but she constituted part of a triad with Ptah and Nefertum during the Middle Kingdom. Thebes was an important cult centre of the triad, which explains the strong presence of Sekhmet in the temples and her depictions in tomb scenes.

This statue represents the goddess Sekhmet as the inscription etched in yellow paint on its base tells us, but on the linen cloth in which the statue is wrapped, we have the inscription: (Harakhty, under the name of Shu, who is in the Aten). Sekhmet here in the shape of a woman with the head of lioness, is sitting on a throne with a low backrest, decorated with feathers and a border of geometrical friezes and on each side of the seat, a square is drawn containing a scene of the *sematawy*, symbol of the unification of Egypt.

The statue is carved of wood with a thick layer of gold leaf; the eyes are inlaid with brown crystal and the muzzle is made from obsidian and another stone.

The goddess is wearing a large solar disk on her head and a smooth tripartite wig from which two braids terminate at breast level; around the neck, a broad *usekh* collar covers the shoulders and chest. She is wearing a tight dress with shoulder straps, decorated with identical geometrical motifs; the dress, which ends at the feet, reveals the breasts and details of the body.

The arms are cut from two separate pieces of wood, which are fixed to the statue's body. The arms at knee level are half bent and slightly raised, the right hand is parallel to the body, it is closed and contains a hollow, which was to hold one of the symbols of divinity of which there remains only one small part. The left hand vertical to the body should hold a sceptre or symbol, which has disappeared today.

THE GOD ANUBIS

Width: 118 cm, length: 270 cm, width: 52 cm.

The wooden statue found at the entry of the treasure room in the tomb of Tutankhamun represents the black jackal god Anubis, guardian of the funerary chamber and the canopic furnishings of the king. The recumbent body lies on a gilded wooden *naos* in the shape of a pylon, assembled on a sledge provided with long carrying poles.

The statue dating from year 8 of Akhenaton's rule was wrapped in linen except for the head, at the time of its discovery. The neck had a long linen scarf with a double blue lotus braid around it.

The statue is plastered and painted black, the funerary colour since he was the god of death, presented thus on the walls of the tombs, but placed here in three dimensions at the entry to the treasury as guardian of all the objects within.

The head of Anubis is menacing; one notices the fineness of the workmanship and the nobility of the animal in the flanks, muscles, legs, muzzle, the pricked ears, the very natural eyes of calcite and obsidian underlined with gold, and the eyebrows. The collar and the scarf are of a very thin sheet of gold. The claws of the animal are silver, which was a very rare and expensive metal at that time.

This statue lies flat on the lid of a shrine divided into several compartments intended to contain some small objects of funerary furniture: four blue earthenware amulets in the form of the back leg of an ox (rebirth), two mummified wooden figurines, blue earthenware statuettes in the image of the baboon god Thoth, god of wisdom, and a god with the head of a falcon, a blue earthenware papyrus-shaped sceptre and jewels. Between the paws of the jackal on top of the shrine, a scribe's palette bears the name of Meretaten, half-sister of Tutankhamun.

The body of the shrine is decorated with an Egyptian throat cornice style moulding of vertical bands round the upper part, a form of decoration, which appeared in the 4th Dynasty and remained in fashion until the Greco-Roman period. The titles of Tutankhamun extend around the shrine, but its principal decoration is a representation of the backbone of Osiris, the *djed* column, symbol of stability, and the tyet knot of Isis, symbol of prosperity and fertility, which are repeated in pairs.

Anubis was a funerary god venerated prior to Osiris, he was the master of the netherworld and the great embalmer, his black colour was the colour of mourning as well as that of the bitumen used in mummification, therefore the colour of rebirth. The Egyptians chose the jackal as their god of mummification, because they were accustomed to seeing this animal running around the necropolis and preying on the mummies. The jackal thus would protect the necropolis and never attack the mummy since he was the protector god.

It was Anubis who was addressed by the deceased in the older mastabas, and it was he who introduced the dead in front of the courts of the judges. He was assimilated with the god Upuaut (the opener of the ways), who was a jackal. Anubis was always carried in funerary processions, and was placed in front of the doorway to the room of the canopic vases to play the role of keeper of the vases. His principal temple was in

old Cynopolis (the City of Dogs) close to Minia. He carried the titles: "Lord of the Necropolis (or the Sacred Land)", "Head of the Sacred House" and "The Highest on the Mountain".

STATUES OF KING TUTANKHAMUN FOUND IN THE CHESTS

Thirty five wooden statuettes standing on rectangular bases of varnished black resin buried with Tutankhamun, were found piled up inside twenty two resin coated wooden *naosoi* with pitched roofs and doors with two batons, assembled on sledges. The *naosoi* are 90,5 cm high, 27 cm in depth and 26,5 cm wide. These statues were distributed between the antechamber and the funerary chamber, but the majority were in the treasury. Registered in yellow on the bases is the forename of King Nebkheperure followed by (beloved…). The statuettes are plastered and gilded from head to toe or alternatively coated with a thick layer of glossy black resin. The religious effectiveness is the same in both cases: black and gold were both associated with regeneration and rebirth.

The statues except for the faces were wrapped in strips of linen; the eyes are painted simply in black encircled with bronze and inlaid with glass and semi-precious materials. The objects which the personages are holding, their sandals and accessories are made of gilded copper. These statues are images of the king or divinities. On the walls of the tombs of Seti II, Amenophis II, Thutmosis IV, Horemheb and Ramses I, statues of this type painted black are represented as ritual figures.

STATUE OF THE KING FISHING WITH A HARPOON ON A PAPYRUS SKIFF

Height: 69.5 cm.

If hunting is known through the reliefs and paintings of the private tombs, it is seldom represented in royal statuary. The two statues of Tutankhamun hunting a hippopotamus are unique; they are carved from wood, which was plastered before being gilded. They show the king sculptured in the round, standing upright on a skiff made from papyrus stems.

The pharaoh is wearing the Red Crown of Lower Egypt, a *usekh* collar and a slightly longer pleated kilt with sandals on his feet. His right leg is slightly raised and he is elegantly balanced on the painted wooden skiff with gilded ends, which stands on a base. The features of the face are very fine; the eyes set in bronze are of obsidian encircled by glass. The king is clasping a bronze harpoon in his right hand and a coil of rope intended for the animal's capture, is in the left. The curved back of the king expresses the movement of floating.

Tutankhamun with his harpoon is hunting an imaginary hippopotamus, the adversary of Osiris and Horus, the gods of good; here he is identified with Horus, king of the gods during his battle with the god Seth, but for reasons of magic the hippopotamus form of Seth is not included in this composition. With his victory over the hippopotamus, which is the bringer of chaos, the pharaoh again creates order in the world.

Hunting the hippopotamus showed that from the time of the Old Kingdom, the king looked after his people and carried out his duties, because it was a fight against the starving animal, which was a great danger to cultivated land.

Such a scene appears on the walls of the temples of Sahure (5th Dynasty) and Pepi II (6th Dynasty), where the hippopotamus is represented much larger than its normal size. During the New Kingdom nobles were also allowed to represent themselves as hunters of hippopotamuses standing in a royal stance.

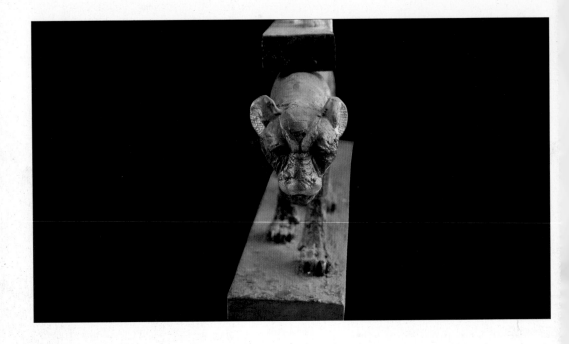

KING TUTANKHAMUN ON A LEOPARD

Total Height: 85.6 cm.

These twin wooden statues represent the pharaoh on a leopard, an animal known for its speed. The king wearing the White Crown of Upper Egypt is holding a *nekhekha* flail in his right hand and a long cane in the other. The head of the king is slightly raised, his glance is fixed, the back straight and the balanced body stable, while the leopard gives the impression of moving.

The royal figure is plastered and gilded, whereas the flail, staff, *uræus* and sandals are of gilded bronze. The eyes and the outline around them are of coloured glass. The base on which the king stands and the animal except for its muzzle, ears and the features around its eyes, are painted black, which contrast with the colour of the sovereign's figure.

These statues symbolized an important stage on the king's journey in the afterlife, during which the deceased king meets the guardians of the skies in human form with the heads of demigods or animals, and with knives in their hands. He will pass quickly through the doors of the skies kept by these demigods, thanks to the speed of the animal, which will prevent them from blocking his path.

As for the symbolism of black, the use of this funerary colour was to instil fear. One can thus imagine the completely gilded deceased passing through the darkness, on an animal invisible due to its black colour with only the muzzle, ears and eyes shining in the gloom of the underworld. The demigods were thus frightened and totally confused seeing the deceased moving past them quickly. The feline is presented moving in a very realistic way; the leopard symbolized the night sky and consequently the kingdom of the netherworld. The pharaoh linked to the sun through the gilding of his body, dominates the leopard exemplifying victory over death.

The two statuettes are however characterized by one essential difference, as while they are both the same size, one of them is in the style of the art of the period of the Aten, characterized by a prominent chest, broad pelvis and low hips; it was suggested at the beginning that it could be a woman, Nefertiti or Kya and that this group was carried out during the Amarna period, but the name of Tutankhamun is engraved on the base of the second statue.

TWO GUARDIAN STATUES OF TUTANKHAMUN

Height 1.75cm, width: 56 cm.

These two imposing life-sized statues true to the dimensions of the king's mummy are called the guardian statues, thanks to their location in the tomb of Tutankhamun. They could also represent two almost identical evocations of King Tutankhamun, the king and his *ka* or most likely two statues of the royal *ka*. The *ka* of the pharaoh was the companion of every moment from his birth until his death, but it returns to find the deceased and divide the goods of the netherworld with him.

The two statues were placed in the passage, which connected the funerary chamber to the antechamber on each side of its sealed entrance. Originally, they were wrapped in pieces of linen, which over time have disintegrated, and very close to each statue there were two bouquets of flowers probably placed there by Tutankhamun's widow during the funeral.

The statues are made from wood painted with a bitumen coloured paint for the flesh, gold leaf for the costumes and bracelets, with the bronze frontal *uræus*, eyebrows, the line which surrounds the eyes and sandals all gilded; and finally an inlay of crystalline limestone and obsidian for the eyes.

The statues are identical except for the headdresses and the text engraved on the kilts. One represents the king wearing a long headdress (*nemes*) over the wig, which falls to frame the neck; the other is differentiated by a funerary headdress (*afnit*) in the form of a headscarf into which all the hair is gathered and released at the neck. On the kilt of the first statue, a text lists some epithets of Tutankhamun: 'Tutankhamun, living forever like Ra each day", while on the other statue the text tells us the name of the royal *ka* of "Horakhty", the name of Osiris, and some names like 'Sovereign, Master of the Two Lands", "The Royal *Ka* of Horakhty", "Osiris Nebkheperure", "Sovereign, Master of the Two Lands, justified".

The king is shown standing, the left leg advanced in a walking stance. His blackened face is very beautiful, the eyebrows and features of the eyes are of gilded bronze, the pupils black, the whites flecked with red in the corners, which looks very natural. On the forehead is the *uræus* symbol of protection. Around the neck, a gilded collar of eight rows made of plaster surmounted by two ribbons, which hang down ending in a pectoral decorated with a winged beetle, which appears to have alighted on his chest.

The king is wearing a gilded kilt with a braided belt and a knot tied under the stomach; it is decorated with the coronation cartouche of King Nebkheperure, "Lord of Existence is the God Ra". The kilt is in the style of the time, pleated tightly behind and covering the front in the shape of a broad triangle. The central part of the triangle is taken up by vertical text, flanked on both sides by four lines of chevron motifs and cobras with the sun disk on their heads. At the two lower corners of the triangle are jackal's heads from which emerge lines like the rays of the sun or pleats of the kilt. This jackal could be the god Anubis, who was always depicted as black and whose role was to guard the necropolis and the tomb, therefore the statue, which was also black achieved the same role.

The king's right hand held perpendicular to the body is holding the handle of a mace with a pear shaped head decorated with scales tightly, while his left hand rests on a papyrus shaped ring on a long staff.

The statue has some protective elements for its journey to the underworld, the frontal *uræus*, mace, staff and sandals, which were symbols of protection in the Pyramids Texts

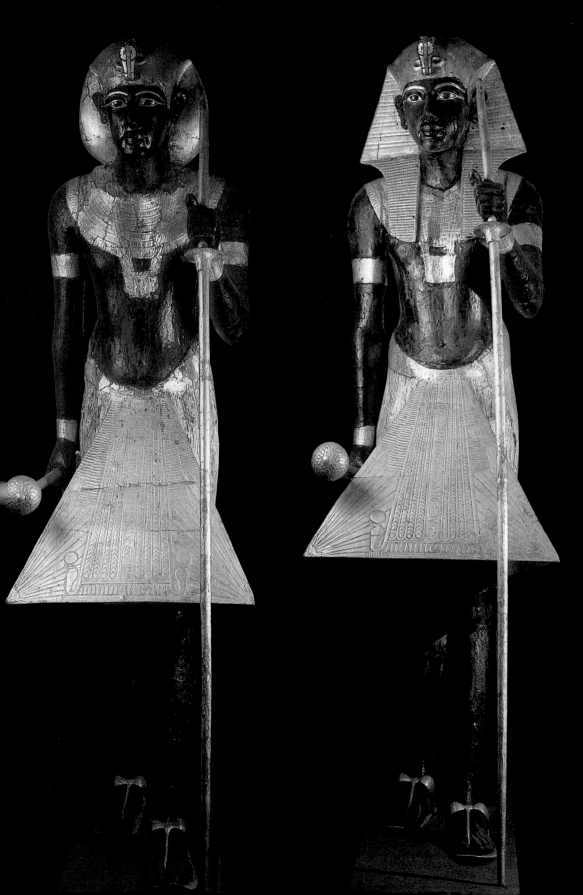

THE GODDESS MENKARET SUPPORTING THE MUMMIFIED KING

This statue was found in the treasury among the statues of King Tutankhamun. It differs from the others because it depicts the figure of a divinity and the king together. The plastered and gilded wooden statue represents Menkaret carrying the mummified king on her head; to facilitate his passage into the afterlife his two feet hang in front of the goddess's face.

Menkaret is in a walking pose with the left foot advanced, she is fully balanced although the back is slightly curved; one hand is supporting the back of the king, while the second is holding his feet up.

King Tutankhamun is wrapped in his mummy bindings. The face is smiling, the eyes defined with a black line. He wears the Red Crown of Lower Egypt and has his arms crossed over his chest.

The goddess is wearing a smooth tripartite wig composed of three sections with long locks of hair, and a dress secured by a shoulder strap trimmed with scales, knotted at the side by a belt with the *tyet* sign on the buckle. The eyes are well defined with black and the ears have bored lobes. Behind the goddess are the *ankh* and *sa* signs, which mean life and protection.

TUTANKHAMUN WEARING THE RED CROWN

Height: 59 cm.

   Among the statues of the king found locked in the trunks in the treasury, these two statues represent the king in a natural pose wearing the Red Crown, the forehead surmounted by a gilded bronze *uræus* and the eyes encircled with an inlay of bronze tinted glass; around the neck is an *usekh* collar, which covers the shoulders and part of the chest and is tied at the nape with two short ribbons.

   The king is standing in a walking position with his left leg forward. The right hand falling parallel to the body is holding a *nekhekh* whip, while the left raised perpendicular to the body is holding a long cane on which the king is leaning. The king's pleated kilt follows the fashion of the time as it covers part of the back and falls in the front to be tied under the stomach forming a pleated section, which stops at the knees.

   The statue shows some characteristics of the art of the Aten period such as ears with pierced lobes, broad bony shoulders, a full chest, protruding belly, pockmarked legs, the head inclined forwards and sandals on the feet.

HEAD OF TUTANKHAMEN EMERGING FROM AN OPEN LOTUS FLOWER

Height: 30 cm

The carved wooden head of Tutankhamen emerging from an open lotus flower is covered by a thin layer of gesso painted brown, with the eyebrows and eyes underlined win blue. It is the masterpiece of King Tutankhamen's tomb, the child's elongated and close-cropped head rises from the open flower; it is a faithful portrait of Tutankhamen at the time of Akhenaton's death.

The dimensions of this head are those of a new-born baby, it bears elements of the period of the Aten when the art form was modified; an elongated rounded head, large ears with pierced lobes, slightly raised, extended eyebrows, wide-open eyes outlined with a line of black, a full face, straight nose, fleshy mouth, small chin and a wrinkled neck.

The lotus, which grew in the marshes of Egypt represented recreation and was a symbol of nobility to the ancient Egyptians. From the beginning of the Old Kingdom, queens and princesses hold it between their fingers as if to smell a sort of divine perfume. The lotus was associated with Nefertum, god of fragrance and the third element of the Memphite Triad made up of the gods Ptah, Sekhmet and Nefertum. The lotus was the god's perfume for the ancient Egyptians and when it accompanied the deceased on his journey to his dwelling in eternity, the anger of the god would immediately fall on the enemies of death.

The ancient Egyptians had three types of lotus, blue, white and pink. The blue was the most sacred because its perfume was light; the white lotus had a stronger scent, so it was not favoured by the priests in the temples of the divinities; the pink lotus imported from India, however was used as an offering.

This flower differs from others because it opens its petals in the morning and closes them again in the evening, it thus brought to mind the god Ra, who disappears in the sky every evening but reappears again each morning under the name of Khepery. The presence of the lotus was an allusion to the birth of the sun as a young royal child. It attested to the fact that the prince was promised kingship.

CHAIRS OF TUTANKHAMUN

In ancient Egypt the chair was a symbol of authority and prestige; the ancient Egyptians had several chair shapes: with a low backrest, which reached halfway up the back, a high backrest, which reached to the nape of the neck, with or without an armrest, and folding chairs.

The material used for the manufacture of the seats was wood of especially good quality imported from Lebanon or Punt (an undefined country located to the south or south-east of Egypt, which had a shoreline on the Red Sea in either Africa or Asia), or Egyptian wood like sycamore, tamarix, palm tree or acacia.

The excavators discovered six chairs and twelve stools in the antechamber and annex of Tuthankhamun's tomb, all of them remarkable. The chairs are brilliant in concept, and the stools form a collection of designs favoured during the New Kingdom.

EPISCOPAL OR CEREMONIAL CHAIR

Height: 102 cm, width; 70 cm, depth: 44 cm, length of the stool: 58.7 cm.

Superbly decorated chair made from ebony wood inlaid with ivory, gold, multicoloured semi-precious stones and faience. It was found knocked over in the south-eastern angle of the annex, wrapped in a strip of linen like the throne, which was astonishing for such a piece.

This chair is a *chef d'œuvre* of the Cairo Museum thanks to its inlay work. It has an unusual form of a folding stool, which was transformed into a seat with a backrest; the beautiful backrest is entirely decorated with ebony, ivory inlays, semi-precious stones and faience, all on a base of gold leaf.

The backrest is the central piece; the top of the scene is crowned by a frieze of *uræi* each surmounted by a solar disk to give protection to the king sitting on the throne. This frieze is broken by a solar disk, which was probably a disk of the Aten in the beginning, but its rays were hidden by a sheet of gold leaf on which empty cartouches were engraved.

Below this frieze, the goddess vulture spreads her wings and holds a fan and a *shen* ring in each claw, thus offering eternity to the king; she is flanked on each side by two cartouches with the royal names of Tutankhamun and Nebkheperure. The lower part is divided into two horizontal friezes of inscriptions, and four vertical bands with inscriptions containing the two cartouches of Tutankhamun.

The seat is curved to take a cushion; it resembles the body of a spotted animal, a cow or an Arabian ibex with its ivory inlays. This seat is attached to a folding stool, which was held in its open position by two wooden supports at the back of the seat, bearing the name of Tutankhamun. The chair's feet are of ebony decorated with sections of ivory and gold leaf, which end in beautiful duck heads two on each side, which are resting on two bars. Between the two sets of feet is a decoration representing the unification of Egypt or the *sematawy*, it was partially damaged by robbers who wanted to remove the gold.

The stool found at the side is also of wood, it is plated and decorated with ebony and coloured glass paste inlays, its surface surrounded by a geometrical frieze is made up of blue and red squares and divided into two parts by a frieze of text written in black on an ivory base.

The two parts are occupied by figures of the nine enemies of Egypt, all bound and dressed in white, with their bows, represented under the sandals of the king, symbol of his authority and victory. They are the Temehu, Nehesu, Restiu, Medjay, Tehenu, Sdjetiu, Wawat, Retenu and Amu. The text which accompanies the scene is: (All the large foreign lands of Asia are forever one (small) thing beneath your sandals, like Ra).

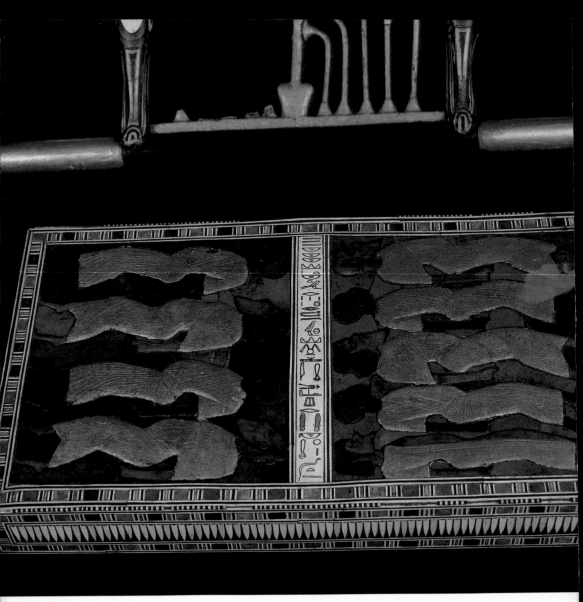

THRONE OF TUTANKHAMUN

Height of chair: 104 cm, length of stool: 63.5 cm.

A *chef d'œuvre* of the Egyptian Museum and the only object that depicts the pharaoh beneath the rays of the Aten. It was made for an adult not a child and was probably Akhenaten's throne, which was used for the crowning of the new King Tutankhamun, so that he appeared on the throne of his father. This throne was wrapped in black linen strips and placed in the antechamber, underneath the hippopotamus bed in the tomb of Tutankhamun.

This throne is a finely worked wooden armchair, covered with silver and gold leaf, inlaid with colour tinted ivory, faience, semi-precious stones like lapis lazuli, cornelian and turquoise, and translucent calcite. The feet of the throne of an imaginary animal are initially connected by an openwork pattern with the *sematawy* symbol (union of the two lands), the feet are of leonine type, a theme which one finds with protective lions that show up on previous feet; they have eyes inlaid with white quartz and crystal.

The point of this throne lies in the inclined backrest, where the inlaid decoration shows us a scene associated with the court at Amarna during the last years of Akhenaten.

The scene on the backrest represents an isolated pavilion with pillars covered with floral patterns and a cornice decorated with *uræi*, and flowers opening in the rays of the sun god the Aten, flanked by cartouches bearing the names of King Tutankhamun as they were written towards the end of Akhenaten's reign. The king is wearing the *atef* crown composed of a number of feathers, conical in shape and with a great number of serpents, each surmounted by a solar disk; the crown is inlaid with coloured glass paste.

The whole of this headdress is surmounted by a short wig, fitted with a diadem with a *uræus* at the front and two fabric ribbons floating at the nape of the neck. Around the neck and covering the shoulders and chest is a broad *usekh* collar inlaid with rows of coloured glass paste. The face and body of the king are inlaid with red cornelian, except for the long pleated kilt attached by a long belt tied under the stomach, with two hanging ribbons partly hiding the *sematawy* on a side of the chair on which the king sits comfortably, resting one arm on the backrest and the other on his knees. The feet of the king are resting on a stool; it is noticeable that one of the sandals is damaged or lost.

The king is looking directly at his wife Queen Ankhsenamon standing with slightly bent back in front of him, wearing a headdress with two long feathers and a circle of *uræi* and narrow horns. The queen's short wig is inlaid with lapis lazuli and provided with a frontal *uræus;* it has been trimmed so that the two ribbons once floating at the back are no longer there.

The queen is wearing a broad collar, which covers the shoulders and part of the chest and a long pleated robe ending at her feet that reveals the details of her body. This robe is knotted under the chest by a long belt whose two ribbons fall the length of her body. The queen is applying perfume to the body of her young husband from a pot, which she is holding in her left hand, one of her sandals is also missing. Behind the wife is posed a high pedestal table inlaid with coloured glass paste, surmounted by a round bouquet made up of several rows of flowers.

The armrests with openwork panels are embellished with winged snakes wearing the Double Crown of Upper and Lower Egypt. These snakes, which are posed on the *neb* sign are inlaid with semi-precious materials and coloured glass paste; between their wings are posed the *shen* sign, symbol of eternity, the two *nesut* and *biti* signs and the cartouche of the king resting on the *nub* sign contain his name in its earlier form with Aten. These snakes symbolize the union of the two protective goddesses. On the right and left, two small snakes wear the White Crown made of silver.

The reverse of the backrest is covered with gold leaf, surmounted by a frieze of lotus and mandrake; it is decorated with an aquatic scene, made up of papyrus plants and flying ducks, which symbolizes love of nature. Also decorating the reverse are four *uræi* each surmounted by a gilded solar disk, and inlaid with coloured glass paste.

Certain details have undergone changes, like the finery which covers the royal couple and which partially masks the rays of life emanating from the Aten disk. The texts on both sides of the couple thus list the couple by their Amun names, therefore in a modified form. On the back of the throne and the armrests, the original names of the king and his wife are engraved. These alterations are probably related to the transformation to which the throne was subjected before being deposited in the tomb.

The stool was laid across the seat, which is inlaid with a checked pattern. It is carved from wood that was plastered and gilded, on which are depicted six bows and three Libyan and three Asian enemies of Egypt being trampled under the king's feet, a symbol of victory. The hieroglyphic text says: (All the important foreign lands of Retenu are under your sandals). On the two sides of the stool are representations of *rekhyt* birds, which surmount the *neb* sign (all) close to the blessed star, meaning to adore, symbolizing the Egyptian people, the text says: (The king is adored by all the people).

CHAIR DECORATED WITH THE GOD HEH

Height, 96 cm, width: 47.6 cm, depth: 50.8 cm.

Gracious chair of a remarkable style discovered in the antechamber of the tomb of Tutankhamun, lacking the splendour of the throne and the ceremonial chair, but none the less it has elegance and style.

This chair is made from an unidentified kind of wood with a very fine grain, assembled with tenons and mortises reinforced by rivets made of a copper alloy topped with a gold head, with the parts covered by very fine gold leaf. The backrest is the centrepiece, it is surmounted by a winged solar disk, which represents Horus, god of *behdet*, around which is a frieze of hieroglyphics listing the king's names and titulary. The centre of the frieze is decorated with a representation of Heh, god of eternity surmounted by a solar disk flanked by two *uræi*, holding in one hand, palm branches whose ends comprise a solar disk and a snake, and with the *ankh* sign passing over the other arm. The god Heh is kneeling on the *nub* hieroglyph meaning (gold). The correlation of these signs together, guarantees the king the hope of a long and prosperous life. On the right and left of the god Heh, columns of engraved texts are surmounted by a falcon wearing the double crown and preceded by a snake. The seat is curved and the parts connecting the feet to the chair are decorated with the *sematawy* sign of the unification of the two lands, formed by the papyrus and the lotus, the symbolic plants of Egypt, from which the stems are missing today. The feline style feet with ivory claws

rest on rounded blocks of wood. Gold leaf covers some parts of the chair: the winged solar disk, the brackets placed at the angle between the seat and the backrest, the *sematawy* emblem in the openwork decoration between the chair's feet.

CHAIR WITH DUCK HEADS

Length: 47 cm, Width: 31,7 cm, height: 34.3 cm.

It is more like a stool, a small chair without a backrest, its use being very widespread in Egyptian houses. During the New Kingdom the stools were folding and their seats were made from leather or fur. With time another style of false stool appeared decorated with fake animal skins.

This stool was found in the antechamber of the tomb of Tutankhamun; manufactured out of ebony, its tilted seat is covered by an imitation skin of a spotted cow made by using ivory inlays.

The tail of the animal ending in an ivory tuft hangs to one side. Each side was equipped with gold paws or claws, which were removed by robbers later on because of the value of the material.

The feet of the stool with the neck of a wild duck, are inlaid with ivory with open beaks from which appears a tongue flecked with pink. They end in crosswise bars. Some parts of the feet and bars are covered with gold leaf in a good state of preservation. The footrest, which does not belong to the stool, is of ebony with ivory inlays.

CEREMONIAL CHARIOT

Height: 118 cm, length: 250 cm.

The chariotry, the corps of the nobility constituted the most powerful part of the Egyptian army; chariot drivers came from the highest ranks, these officers acquired the culture of the scribes as well as military training, the most gifted succeeded to the highest duties: military chiefs, governors and ambassadors. The king's own sons assumed the duties of (first driver of the pharaoh's chariot) and (director of horses).

Chariots appeared during the 18th Dynasty as an element borrowed by the Egyptians from Asia Minor; they were associated with the king during the battles of the New Kingdom. On murals and reliefs, chariots were represented as diplomatic gifts in the Amarna letters. Before the discovery of the tomb of Tutankhamun, only two chariots had been brought to light, one of which came from the tomb of Tuya and Yuya No (46) in addition to a whole set of accessories, which was found in the tombs in the Valley of the Kings.

The Egyptian chariot consisted of a light open box called a body where the pharaoh stood; it rested on two wheels, the back was decorated with a palm leaf shape, spirals and animals of Asian origin and what is remarkable is that gold predominated in the chariots of the kings and nobles. This box was equipped with a pole to which two horses were harnessed; the harness of the horses was composed of a snaffle bit with a noseband, a cockade on the head with feathers, a collar made up of a broad strap for the withers, another tight strap across the horse's chest and finally the reins.

The team was composed of a driver and a warrior; the Egyptian chariot carried two men: the driver who held a whip often a luxury item and the warrior armed with a bow. Two holders filled with javelins and arrows were attached to the sides of the case of the chariot's body. The pharaoh is represented alone on his chariot, the reins are attached around his pelvis to free his hands to handle the bow or lance, thus he drove the chariot by moving his hips.

Carter discovered the dismantled parts of six large complete chariots in the tomb, rich and refined, piled up pell-mell along the eastern wall of the antechamber within the tomb. Two of a larger size, undoubtedly ceremonial, a smaller highly decorated one and three others made of light material for daily use. The vehicles were dismantled at the time of the funeral because of their large dimensions, which would have prevented them from passing through the narrow access corridor. The incredible disorder in which Carter found the chariot parts was due to the passing of robbers in search of easily transportable valuable items. The state of the chariots' bodies was satisfactory and it was possible to reassemble them.

The sumptuous ceremonial chariot is made of wood covered with gold leaf. The external decoration of the body is made out of artificially bent wood, covered with plaster and gilded; it is composed of a pattern of spirals broken in the centre by a lotus column, surmounted by cartouches containing the pharaoh's forename, name and Horus name.

The internal decoration is very finely worked, it extends to three levels; on the upper register, the cartouches of Tutankhamun, in the centre is the *sematawy* heraldic emblem of the union of Upper and Lower Egypt, the lower register, represents a shackled prisoner on each side. A frieze at the bottom shows a number of bound foreign prisoners, Nubian, Asian and Libyan, kneeling in front of the king with the features of a triumphant royal sphinx, represented on the two sides and crushing his enemies.

The deck was made of think interwoven leather strips on which animal skins or woven linen were laid. At each end of this platform, the head of the god Bes as a deformed dwarf with a protruding tongue is represented; his head is surmounted by a headdress in the form of a cylindrical pot decorated with coloured glass paste inlays in blue and brown, his eyes are inlaid with crystal. The six wooden spokes of the wheels are encircled with leather and covered with gold, while the yoke is connected to the pole, its two ends carry representations of prisoners, an Asian and a Nubian, and these would have rested on the necks of the two horses. The chariot is provided with some elements to ensure the driver's protection: the representation of the god Horus, a winged solar disk, the royal lions, the god Bes and two cobras.

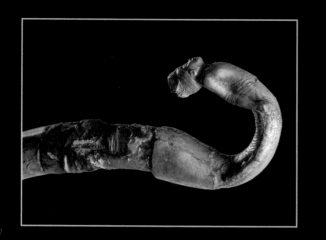

ACCESSORIES OF THE CEREMONIAL CHARIOT

The chariots of the king had been dismantled, but it was easy to put them back together thanks to their good state of preservation. Fittings were found beside the chariots, some have been fixed to the body of the chariots, but others are on show beside these chariots in the showcases.

For example, the blinkers of the horses of the king's ceremonial chariot, which bear the well drawn representation of the eyes of Horus, with the eyebrows parallel to the black line of the eyes. The decoration also consists of a lotus flower inlaid with coloured glass paste of blue, green, white and red. The blinkers are decorated with a line of circles with multi-coloured inlays.

Other accessories carry the representation of the god Bes in the round or in relief. He takes the form of a fearsome dwarf opening the mouth as if screeching to frighten the enemies, and at the same time protecting the king driving the chariot from the bites of snakes, and insects and bad spirits. He has big ears, a large beard and a headdress in the form of a lotus flower inlaid with coloured glass paste. On other parts Bes is represented in relief wearing a headdress of coloured feathers.

The chariot's pole is a thin stick attached to the body, it ends in two slanted yokes; this yoke is attached to the neck of the horses by a rope; the artist put a representation of the king's enemies, bound Asians or Nubians upon this yoke, as a symbol of the king's victory.

On one piece of equipage, one can also see the image of the god Horus in the round, with beautiful eyes inlaid with obsidian. He is standing on a pedestal and his head is surmounted by a large solar disk carrying a scene in relief, which shows the name of King Nebkheperure with a large winged scarab surmounted by the solar disk and flanked by two *uræi* each of whom wears the double crown, and from which hang two *ankh* signs. Between the scarab and the solar disk, three *ankh* and two *was* signs are depicted.

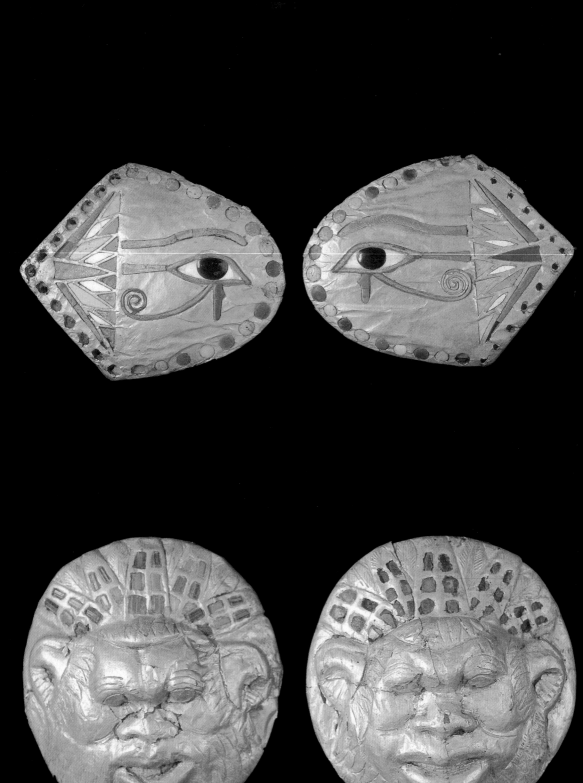

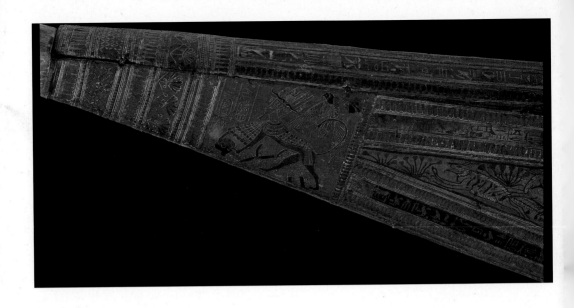

WOODEN BOX CONTAINING BOWS

Length: 153 cm.

A beautiful box found in a corner of the treasury containing three examples of a type of Asian composite bow, which was introduced into Egypt before the reign of Tutankhamun. This wooden box is covered with plaster and fabric, decorated with scenes and marquetry in coloured woods and leather flecked with green.

The ends of the box have faience lion's heads, followed by several rows of ivory inlays on a wooden base, then a scene representing the king as a sphinx trampling on Asian and Nubian enemies. The king here is wearing a trimmed false beard, a composite *atef* crown with a number of feathers, solar disks and *uræi*. Behind the king, a winged falcon is flying and holding the *shen* symbol of eternity.

Each side is divided into three main parts; the middle contains a wrought gold panel depicting the pharaoh standing fully balanced on the chariot, drawn by two well decorated galloping horses. Tutankhamun holding a bow in his hand is hunting animals, which are fleeing in front of the chariot, helped by his hunting dog.

To the right and left are animated inlaid panels of dogs, game animals and wild beasts such as hares, gazelles, wild asses and leopards, all wounded by the pharaoh's arrows; these too are surrounded by plants and shrubs. The inscriptions on the box giving the pharaoh's names and titles occupy the spaces between the panels.

SHIELD

Height: 88cm, width: 55 cm.

Weapons were known to the Egyptians from Pre-dynastic times; they were made of stone or copper: like the jet staff, which was useful for hunting or to reach a distant enemy, the bow, the club, the axe and shields, which were weapons of defence. But weaponry completely changed at the beginning of the New Kingdom, following the campaigns to drive out the Hyksos the war chariot made its appearance, the broadsword that the gods gave to the king became a symbol of victory and bronze replaced copper. The king donned the blue helmet or crown of war, while the soldiers wore helmets and carried round shields and lengthened broadswords.

The first examples of shields date from the Old Kingdom; they were round being made from the carapaces of tortoises, which were then covered with cow hide and called *ikm*. The clearance of the antechamber brought to light eight shields; according to Howard Carter this one was for ceremonial use.

This shield is made of wood plated with gold, it is rectangular with an arched top; on the top is the traditional representation of the winged solar disk representing protection and blessing. The legend of the solar disk tells us that having overcome his uncle Seth, Horus was immediately transformed into a winged solar disk, which was always represented in the temples and tombs. This same solar disk would be responsible for protecting the passage of the god Ra against the enemies, who would try to prevent the appearance of the solar disk each morning, the same as for life on earth because the winged solar disk would protect humanity, the deceased in his tomb, the divinities in their temples and the people.

In the centre of the shield, Tutankhamun in a traditional pose is represented in a victorious attitude wearing the *atef* crown surmounted by two ram's horns with feathers, in the middle are two smaller horns enclosing the solar disk. Beneath the crown, a short wig is attached to his forehead by a ribbon whose two ends float behind his neck. The king is wearing a short false beard, a pearl collar and bracelets on his forearms; his transparent robe, which reveals all the details of the body, is tied just below the stomach using a long belt, imitating those worn during the Amarna period, and he is wearing sandals on his feet.

The king's raised right hand is holding the *khepesh* sword; in his other, he is gripping an animal by the tail; it is a lion, which characterized the enemies of the country. This animal has only one tail, eight legs and two heads, the artist probably wanted to represent movement in the animal's body.

Behind the king, Nekhbet, the vulture goddess of the south, originating in Nekheb (El Kab) in Upper Egypt, is represented on a stem of papyrus wearing a white *hedjet* crown. She is spreading her wings to protect and give the life to the pharaoh, like the goddess Isis who spread her wings beneath the nose of Osiris to give him the breath of the life. She is holding the *nekhakha* flail behind her back and the *shen* symbol of eternity is between her wings.

Opposite the head of Tutankhamun can be seen hieroglyphic inscriptions noting the relationship between Montu, god of war and the king to prove his strength as a warrior king: "Beneficent god, with a powerful arm, unwavering heart, the image of Montu in the heart of Thebes, who fights lions and destroys wild beasts". The king is trampling on the *khasut* sign signifying foreign lands, symbol of submission by the enemies.

IRON DAGGER AND SHEATH

Length of knife: 34.2 cm.

Two daggers were discovered in the tomb of Tutankhamun, this one being of iron and the other of gold; they were found in the wrappings of the king's mummy.

The iron dagger was attached to a belt, which was inserted against the left thigh. Iron did not exist in Egypt at this time but its use was widespread in Asia and it was used by the Hittites in their weaponry.

This example is as important as the gold one; its iron blade carries no decoration or incisions, but the handle is richly incised with zigzag motifs realised in gold and between these lines are geometrical and floral forms of inlays of coloured glass and semi-precious materials. As for the pommel at the hilt of the knife, it is made of rock crystal and is in a very fine style.

The sheaths of the two daggers are made of gold; that of the iron one is decorated on one side with a feather motif finishing near the point with a head of a jackal with long ears, which probably denotes the god Anubis. Its role here was to ensure protection of the deceased. The other side has a lotus pattern.

CANES

Canes and staffs were symbols of nobility; these were found in a long box under the bed of Tutankhamun in the antechamber of his tomb. They are made from different materials: ivory, ebony, wood covered with gold, faience and cornelian; all bear the name of the king.

The canes were made in such a way as to present the body of one or more prisoners, enemies or slaves, head down. These type of scenes of prisoners are usually on top of the stools placed under the feet of the kings, being counted or killed in front of the gods, as a symbol of submission. The usage of these sticks was different to that of today as they were not made simply to be held in the hand to crush the enemy, but also as a seal in the name of Tutankhamun due to the royal cartouche at the base of the staff on the lotus flower.

Engraving on the sticks was carried out in two ways: either by incising the wood covered with a layer of plaster, then applying gold leaf onto the incisions, or by covering the stick with a fine material, engraving it, and finally removing this layer; the reason for the layer was to prevent the sheet of gold leaf from tearing during the process.

CANE WITH AN ASIAN

Length: 109 cm.

This cane is no different from any other in shape, but it carries a decoration of an Asian on its slanting part. It is made of ebony with no decoration except for the exposed parts of the body such as the hands and face, which are of ivory to denote the pale colour of Asians. The prisoner's robe of the same colour as the wood, is tight and long and furnished with incisions.

His head is a masterpiece despite its small size, his hair is covered with a skullcap, his long thick beard is painted black, his eyes are open and the eyebrows are drawn with a black line, there is a slight smile on the lips. The prisoner's hands are tied at the sides, and his feet are tied to the back of the body.

CANE WITH A NUBIAN

Length: 102 cm.

The name Nubia may be a modification of the Egyptian name *nub*, which means gold. Nubia is a country located to the south of Egypt between Aswan and North Sudan; it is divided into two parts and both have been linked to one another by the Nile, trade and warfare since remote times. Nubia became an Egyptian possession during the 18th Dynasty, having an Egyptian governor who sent booty to Egypt each year. This wooden cane with a tilted handle is the representation of a Nubian enemy. The two arms and hands are tied behind the back so as to restrict all movement; the other end of the cane is in the form of a lotus made of blue glass. The Nubian is carved in a dark black wood, which is ebony; the head is engraved with the characteristic features and frizzy hair of the Nubians.

CANE DECORATED WITH TWO PRISONERS; A NUBIAN AND AN ASIATIC

Length: 104 cm.

The traditional enemies of Egypt were the Nubians, Asians and Libyans; royal power was affirmed by showing these people being humiliated. On the cane's handle two enemies, a Nubian and Asian are bound together by their feet and hands. The bare parts of the Nubian's body are of ebony with inlays and colours for the short sleeved robe and the headband, his hair is frizzy and the lips are thick. The body of the Asian is of ivory and his clothes are different, the robe is ornamented with circular patterns and has long sleeves fitted with ribbons, which cross over the chest.

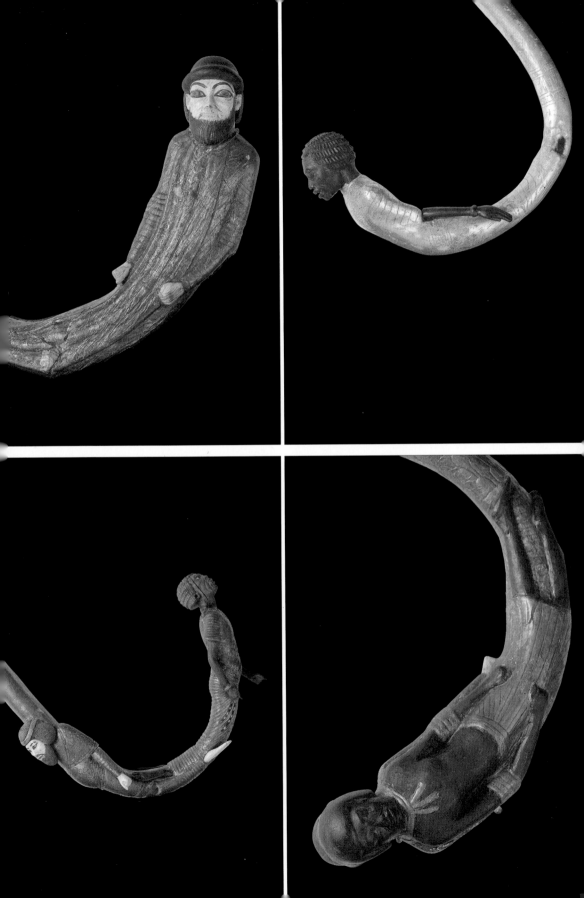

SCEPTRES

Insignias of royalty and divine power that can be called sceptres were numerous. The gods rest on the *was* a stick ending in a small fork at the bottom and in a head of stylized greyhound (saluki) at the top, which evokes the animal of Seth. This sceptre was the ensign of the nome of Thebes, which bore the name Waset (The city of the sceptre).

The magic sceptre of the goddesses was the papyrus stem, similar to the papyriform column; its name wadj means greenery and symbolizes eternal youth.

In official representations, the king is shown holding the *heka* sceptre and *nekhekh* flail tightly against his chest, symbols of Osiris borrowed from the primitive divinity Andjty of Busiris. This protection is represented in the primitive emblems of the nomes, as a shepherd with a crook (the *heka*), and the flail (the *nekhekh*). The symbolism is clear, the king is the shepherd of his people whom he leads and protects with the flagellum (the root of *nekhekh*).

The king retains some other attributes of power, these are the *khereph* sceptre, which was at the beginning a mace with a cylindrical head and also the mace with a pear or pyriforme head. In the New Kingdom, Amun gives the king the *khepesh*, which is the curved sword, as a token of victory,

CROOK

Length: 33.5 cm.

A symbol of royal authority, which appeared later carried by Osiris the god of the afterlife, who carries it thanks to his quality as a divine king. As for the sovereign, he carried it during his coronation and the *sed* festival, thus marking the renewal of his power.

This sceptre was found in a chest in the antechamber, and was probably held in the king's hands during his coronation in Tell el-Amarna; this point of view is supported by an inscription on the base of the crook, which contains the two cartouches of the pharaoh with his name as Tutankhaten and not Tutankhamun.

The crook's rod is composed of alternating cylinders in blue glass paste and gilded metal on a bronze framework. This sceptre was compared to a shepherd's crook because the hieroglyphic sign of this insignia means (to direct).

SCEPTRE

Length: 54 cm.

This sceptre can have the following names *sekhem* (the powerful one), *kherep* (that which directs), and *aba* (that which commands). Each had a role, but during the ceremonies it was difficult to distinguish which insignia it was.

High dignitaries generally used the *kherep*. This one was discovered in the annex, it could be the *aba* generally associated with the ritual offerings.

The upper part of the sceptre is decorated with a large frieze with *hekeru* and geometrical motifs, and on one of the two faces, an inscription: (The Beneficial God, the Well-beloved whose face shines like the Aten, the Son of Amun, Nebkheperure, who has received the gift of eternal life). The Aten is called upon here as a god of the Egyptian pantheon. This text could have been written at the time of the abandonment of Tell el-Amarna. On the second face, a scene of a ritual sacrifice of oxen is divided into five panels.

The decoration of the sceptre's staff is splendid; the two ends have a decoration of feathers inlaid with glass paste of various colours. Its upper end is a papyrus flower with an umbel, inlaid with turquoise, cornelian, lapis lazuli and glass paste. The inscription is written in gold on a blue faience ground; the wooden sceptre is covered with thick sheet of gold leaf. The lower end takes the shape of an open papyrus plant.

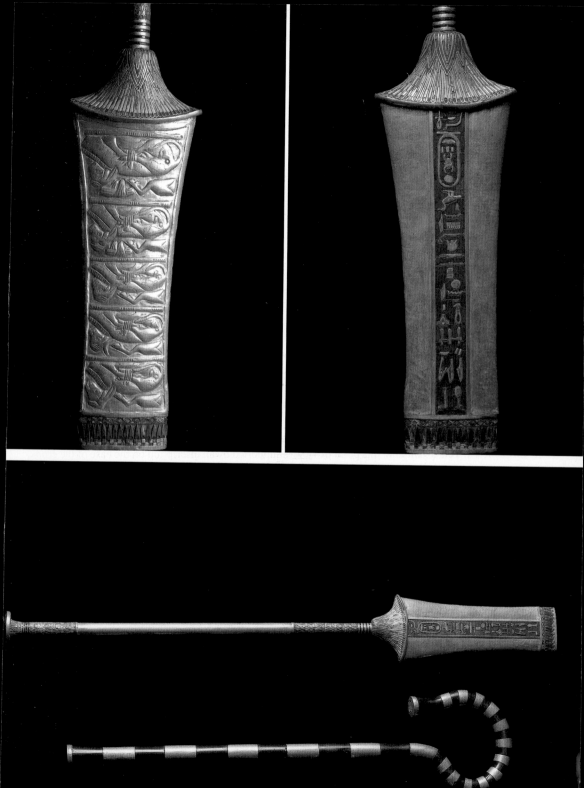

UNGUENT BOX

Height: 16 cm, width: 8.8 cm, depth: 4.3 cm.

A double unguent box discovered at the bottom of the large sarcophagus inside which, Carter found a quantity of brown powder with an unpleasant odour; it is probably a scented paste, which was used as an unguent. This box had a funerary use, which explains the place where it was discovered, very close to the mummy in the funerary room.

The box is made of wood covered with gold leaf inlaid with coloured glass paste and semi-precious stones like turquoise and cornelian. Each of the boxes is in the form of a cartouche, the two were placed side by side and each of their lids are in the form of a solar disk surmounted by two long feathers with inlays of red, dark blue and turquoise blue glass paste. They both rest on a silver base, which has an engraved decoration formed by the two signs of the *ankh* and *was*.

These two boxes are symbolic, they bear three scenes, the two on the front and the back are surrounded by a frieze inlaid with dark blue glass paste; the third which occupies the sides is engraved on gold leaf without any inlay. The three scenes show a man sitting on the jubilee *sed* symbol, which has the shape of a large basket containing in the middle a cartouche surrounded by lines. The accessories and clothes of each man differ from one scene to another.

On the front, the cartouches contain images of the young king during his childhood with the lock of youth hanging to one side, which are inlaid with lapis lazuli. Next to the hairstyle is a ribbon, which descends and floats on the shoulders, the *uræus* on the forehead shows that the king is already reigning.

These representations are surmounted by a large ivory solar disk flanked by two *uræi* from which hang two *ankh* signs. The king is kneeling on the jubilee *sed* sign, which is inlaid with coloured glass paste; the arms crossed on the chest are holding the *heka* and *nekhekh* sceptres. Around the neck, he is wearing a broad *usekh* collar inlaid with coloured glass paste. The king's transparent pleated robe with short sleeves typical of the Amarna period, is tied under the chest, which allows us to see the details of the body like the full belly and swollen thighs.

On the back, the scene shows the king sitting on the *sed* sign wearing the blue crown of war; he is no longer a child but rather a strong and warlike man. Two sceptres are in the palms of the hands resting comfortably on the knees, they are the crook and the flail. One of the representations of the king has a black painted face, probably as a symbol of rebirth, the underworld and the continuity of life.

On the sides of the box, engraved drawings show Heh the god of eternity kneeling on the *sed* sign, holding *renpet* palm tree branches ending in the *shen* and tadpole signs, thus symbolizing a promise of a million years of life for the king, who is reproduced in the two preceding scenes and whose cartouches are to the right and left of the god.

The god Heh is surmounted by the name Nebkheperure written with a large winged scarab surmounted by the solar disk, and resting on the *neb* sign. The god is wearing a tripartite wig, a coiled false beard, a *usekh* collar, a corselet with scales and straps, and a short pleated kilt attached by a belt. From the left hand hangs an *ankh* sign and as regards the right hand, it is simply resting on his knee. To the right and left of the wrinkled neck of Heh and in front of his face, the two cartouches of King Tutankhamun are engraved.

AMULET IN THE FORM OF THE GODDESS WERET-HEKAU

Height: 14.5 cm.

One of the poles of magico religious medicine along with doctors and healing divinities is the power attributed to amulets. From the roots of the hair to the tips of the toes, each part of the alive or mummified body is placed under the protection of a talisman. Amulets exert a primarily protective function and accompany a person from birth to death, and especially in the hereafter.

It was a question of protecting a man from disease, stings and bites. It was also necessary to protect the infant and child, the pregnant woman as well as one giving birth. The amulet offered a magic aid during all stages of life marked by the journey from birth to death, while passing by diseases and voyages, to the changing of the years or seasons. These transitions were regarded as dangerous stages because inherently they represented the unknown, the moment when a weakened man could be taken over by malicious forces.

The form of the amulet, its colour and the material used, met a specific need and the form suggested the symbol with which it was associated; but in Egypt, the pictorial richness of the hieroglyphic vocabulary is such that writing signs were also used as an amulet. The *djed* pillar or the spinal column of Osiris translated the idea of continuance and stability, it is among the amulets known as power; the *ankh* is life, strength, beauty, prosperity and consciousness.

he *wadj* papyrus stem is greenery or energy; the *wadjet* eye of the god Horus the magic eye of protection, symbolizes perfection. The scarab linked to the sun at dawn symbolizing rebirth, was placed on the mummy's chest as a substitute, there was also the *ib* heart and the *tyt* knot of Isis, and the cartouche.

The variety of amulets is infinite, royal emblems, crowns, *uræi*, or divine emblems like the forms of the gods Ptah, Bes, Sekhmet, Thoth, Sobek, Wadjet and Nekhbet. Certain amulets represent hybrid creatures or dangerous animals assigned to drive out bad spirits.

The colour of the amulet is part of its magic function, gold and yellow, which evoke the sun are a symbol of eternity, blue is the colour of renaissance, green of life and all that grows, black denotes the fertility of the Nile silt and white evokes purity.

Materials used for the manufacture of amulets are jasper, hematite, feldspar, lapis lazuli, cornelian, enamelled faience, glass, wood, gold and silver. Magic texts from the Book of Dead were registered on some of them.

Among the a hundred and fifty pieces found between the strips of Tutankhamun's mummy, twenty five were amulets and the majority of them were found in close proximity to the neck.

In a gilded wooden *naos* box discovered in the antechamber decorated with engraved scenes, a bituminized pedestal was brought to light, which still bears the traces of two feet. This pedestal was devoted to a figurine of the king probably in gold, which had already been stolen at the time of the opening of the tomb. Also in the *naos* there were the remains of a ceremonial sash and a statuette wrapped in linen.

This figurine which is not really an amulet is considered so thanks to its role and power, which are undoubtedly magic. It is made of gilded wood, suspended from a collar made of simple gold beads, cornelian, feldspar and glass paste. The goddess's neck and that of the pharaoh as well as his feet are surrounded by small beads of various colours.

The king is suckling at the breasts of the goddess Isis serpent with a human head and breasts and arms; she is called Weret Hekau (the great one of magic), she has a nursing aspect composed of a snake with a female head and a royal headdress with a vulture's feather, a small disk and a crown formed of two large feathers and horns. The headdress is resting on a vulture's skin, which hides part of the smooth tripartite wig, while the vulture's head surmounts the goddess's forehead; around the neck a broad collar with six rows covers the chest. The body of the goddess is coiled on a base of gilded wood and the text registered on this base describes Tutankhamun as (The Beloved of Weret Hekau).

Tutankhamun does not appear as a child but an adult man with the blue *khepresh* crown of war, a broad collar around the neck and a long pleated kilt, whose belt is tied under the stomach; the details of the face and body are typical of the Amarna style. The goddess encircles him with her left arm, while she brings her breast towards him with the other hand.

GILDED BOX CONTAINING STYLUSES

Length: 30 cm.

The position of a scribe in ancient Egypt was a great service or responsibility. The scribe was a highly envied personage because he was from a privileged class throughout the whole of the Egyptian civilization, exempted from taxes and rewarded by the king.

During the Old Kingdom, the career of a scribe was reserved for members of the royal family and the families of the nobles; it was only with the New Kingdom when the pharaohs introduced a kind of state socialism, that the career of a scribe was opened to any Egyptian and he did not have to come from the royal family. Young children had to spend time in the schools of the scribes to be able to read and write.

The scribe occupied several

- positions at the same time; in the fields, he recorded the revenues and imposed taxes; in war, he counted the casualties, the dead and the spoils; in the workshops, he counted the steles, statues and *objets d'art*; in the temples, he recorded the goods and offerings; in the tombs, he counted what the deceased had been responsible for during his terrestrial life; in the workshops, he received the vases and earthenware jars of beer and wine, and he recorded their contents. He was represented in several ways, standing or squatting: perched forward reading his papyrus and writing with an attentive expression listening to the royal decrees.

A scribe's instruments are: a palette with two pots with a case which contains red and black powdered ink, always carried on the shoulders of the scribes in scenes and reliefs, a sheet of papyrus, a burnisher to polish the sheet before using it, a scraper of a kind of very fine limestone to erase mistakes, a broad slate stele on which to fix the sheet to write on and the reed used to write. The first evidence of a scribe was perhaps on the palette of Narmer, but Egyptian history never ceased to save the names and roles of the scribes during the reigns of important kings. This luxurious box was made to contain styluses. Discovered with the other elements necessary to the scribe, it is in the shape of a column surmounted by a palm-shaped capital, formed of palm tree leaves; the abacus forms the lid, which swivels to open. It was closed using two knobs around which a cord was passed.

The lid and two knobs are of ivory while the box is wood; it is gilded with incisions in the form of *hekeru*, fish scales and diamond shapes inlaid with cornelian, obsidian and glass paste. The central part of the box is filled by the two cartouches of King Tutankhamun, each surmounted by two feathers.

Tutankhamun could read and write, and the presence of the necessities of a scribe in his tomb, leads us to think that he could have made use of them or wanted the blessing and protection of the scribes.

SANDALS WITH REPRESENTATIONS OF ENEMIES

Length: 28 cm.

Sandals were called *thebet* by the ancient Egyptians; they comprised a sole, a thin strap, which passed between the big and second toes, two fastenings, which passed under the instep and sometimes a third, enclosing the back of the foot to hold it securely. The sandals were sometimes flat, sometimes with a curved end, usually manufactured out of leather for the living, but generally woven from the leaves of palm trees or papyrus stems for the deceased. The sole was sometimes lined with linen on which the Egyptians liked to have their enemies reproduced, so that they could have the satisfaction of walking on them.

Although sandals were known during the Pre-dynastic period, ancient Egyptian males only wore them on visits and the women never. In the Old Kingdom sandals were seldom worn, kings and dignitaries walked barefoot and had sandal carriers following them, they only donned their sandals if they were presenting themselves to the god. During the Middle Kingdom, it was only the poor who did not have sandals, something that was regarded as a sign of poverty. People held their sandals in their hands and put them on only after having reached the goal of their walk. In the New Kingdom, the use of sandals had spread everywhere, but customs prohibited wearing them in the presence of people of higher rank.

There were also sandals for the religious services, which were represented as symbols of protection in the Pyramids Texts, on sarcophagi and in the text of the Book of the Dead. At the end of the 18th Dynasty, sandals began to appear on the feet of statues. The king had to wear sandals when he climbed into his papyrus enclosure to overcome his enemies in the afterlife, so as to be able to leave for an eternal world.

One thus used sandals only where they were essential, the nobles for their walks outside the house and the servants when they had to run around the fields. As soon as it was possible, the kings and nobles removed their sandals and entrusted them to the 'sandal porters', who followed them.

Sandals were manufactured from organic material, papyrus fibres, palm tree bark or leather. And to make them, the workers softened the leather or the papyrus stems by putting them in large vases filled with water. Then when they had become softer and had the necessary suppleness, they were cut using a sandal shape.

One hundred or so sandals were discovered in the tomb of Tutankhamun in the chests containing clothing or scattered in the antechamber and annex. Sandals of simple papyrus and luxurious ones of leather were found, in addition to those decorated with beads and other patterns. Leather sandals and those with beads have deteriorated or disintegrated, making it impossible to piece them together.

This pair of sandals was never worn; they are made of wood with a decoration engraved into the outside surface, sheets of leather and gold leaf were then applied to the marquetry. The deceased's feet required gold to assist him in the voyage into the afterlife. Two enemies, an Asian and a Nubian tied back to back with their eight bows, are represented to be crushed under the king's feet, when he puts on the sandals.

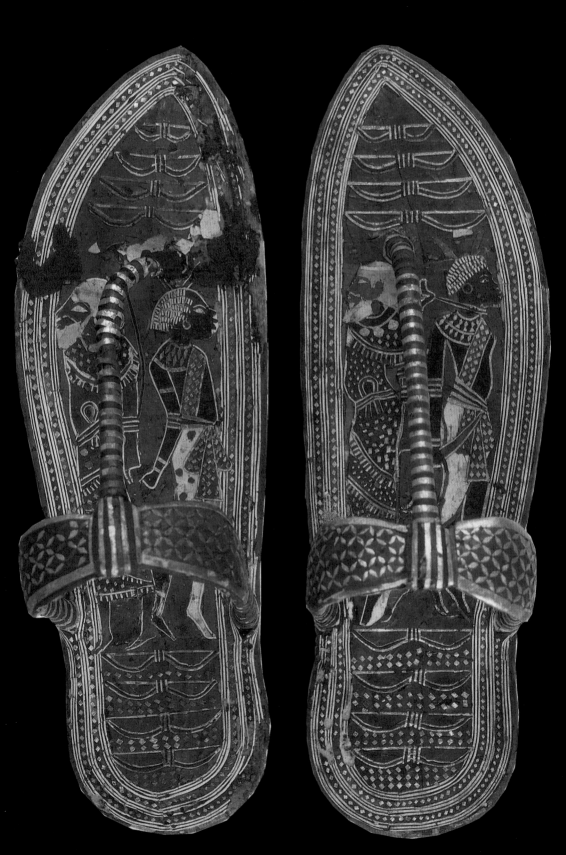

MIRROR CASE DECORATED WITH THE GOD HEH

Height: 26.8 cm, width: 14.2 cm.

Mirrors were major elements in the funerary furniture of the ancient Egyptians; among the names for mirrors the word *ankh*, which means life, and the materials used in its manufacture were silver and bronze.

This case is considered of value because of the new shape and decorative representations, which ornament it. Found in a chest in the treasury of the tomb of Tutankhamun, it is manufactured of wood and is formed of right and left sides placed one above the other; the case is empty, the mirror undoubtedly made of precious materials is lost, while the ivory handle in the shape of a floral stem with an inscription, was discovered in another chest. The shape of the case is very unusual as it is in the form of a kneeling man, Heh, god of infinity, who ensures eternal life for the king; he wears a smooth tripartite wig, a plaited false beard, a *usekh* collar on the chest, bracelets, a corselet decorated with scales and a pleated kilt with a belt knotted around the waist.The god Heh raises his two arms, which hold two serrated palm tree branches, which are the *renpet* or years' sign ending in tadpoles, posed above the *chen* sign, which means a hundred thousand years. To the right and left of Heh are two of the king's cartouches, one of the birth and one of the crowning.

The head of Heh is surmounted by an almost round shape, which probably held the mirror possibly made of silver that has disappeared today. The eyes of the god are inlaid with white limestone and obsidian, a blue line indicates the eyes, eyebrows and false beard.

On the front of the case, a version of the first name of Pharaoh Nebkheperure is engraved with a winged scarab surmounted by a solar disk. On the back, the same name is written in a cartouche surmounted by a

solar disk placed on the *nub* sign for gold. It is encircled by two *uraei*, one wearing the Red Crown, the other the White. The case is covered with a sheet of red gold except for the branches of the palm tree, the tadpoles and the *chen* signs, which are in a bright yellow gold

BRONZE TRUMPET

Length: 49.4 cm.

Musical instruments in ancient Egypt fell into several categories, such as percussion like the drum and tambourine, action like sistrums, castanets and clappers, string like the harp and lyre, and wind like the trumpet and flute.

The trumpet was called *sheneb* in ancient Egyptian; it was primarily used during military campaigns often in partnership with a drum, during parades or to sound the rallying cry of the soldiers. The first known representations of a trumpet date from the New Kingdom.

The treasure of King Tutankhamun contains two splendid trumpets, which were placed inside the funerary room and in the south western angle of the first gilded chapel. The trumpet with its sound was to awaken the king for the million jubilees. The first is made of silver and gold, the second of gold and bronze with the centre piece of ebony.

The two trumpets of the king together with one in the Louvre Museum are the only sound instruments, which let us hear a voice from antiquity. They can produce high pitched and bass notes.

The bronze trumpet measures ten centimetres less than the silver trumpet; the bronze is partially covered with gold. This trumpet is composed of a silver ring, tube and bell. On the bell, King Tutankhamun is depicted wearing the blue *khepresh* crown with in his hand a curved *heka* sceptre, symbol of authority, in front of the mummified god Ptah in his chapel. He is receiving the ankh of life from the god Amun-Ra in the presence of the falcon god Ra-Horakhty. The decoration is a religious rather than military.

Each trumpet has a wooden core, undoubtedly intended to protect the instrument. Most of the time, the scenes on the trumpet represent two men, one blowing the instrument while the other salutes the troops while wedging the trumpet's core under his arm then putting it back inside the trumpet after use.

Egyptian trumpets had several roles, they announced the arrival of the king and the opening of festivals, they were used to banish bad spirits with the production of a musical sound and they appeared in military representations of the New Kingdom, especially in the hands of military guards on the walls of the tombs in Tell el-Amarna. During the Ramesside period, trumpets directed the dressage of the pharaoh's horses, which appear to dance to the sound of the trumpet.

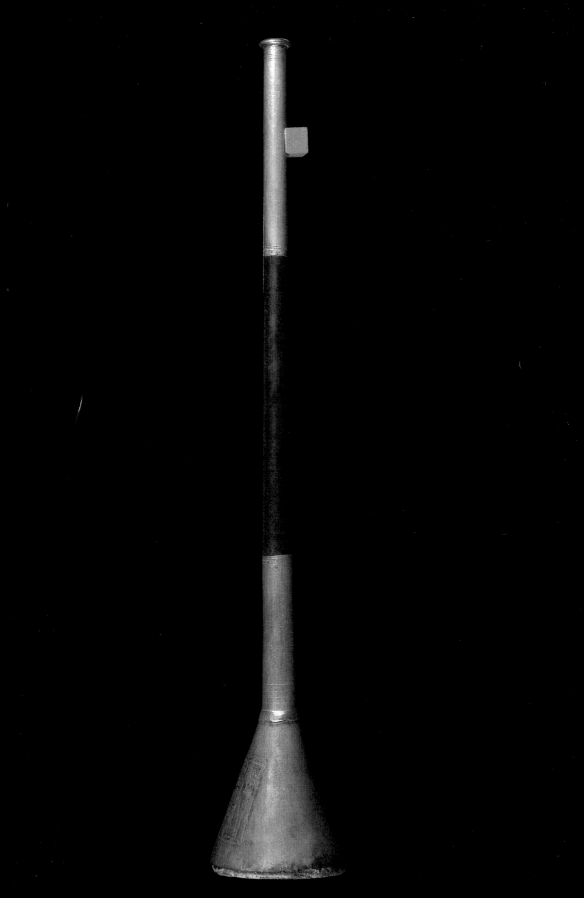

BOATS

Barques and boats were the most important means of transport in a country like Egypt, where the river is the essential link between the north and south. The ancient Egyptians had several kinds of barques, those which are simple for hunting and fishing, promenade boats, funerary barques, divine boats used during the festivals devoted to the divinities, pilgrimage barques used for the mummies, the solar *mendjet* barques, the *mesketet* night boats, boats to transport goods, people and obelisks and boats of war or the maritime fleets.

The boats are manufactured of wood or papyrus reeds; the sails, the rudders and oars with the ropes of flax, were major elements.

These boats are made up of three essential parts: the prow, the poop and the hull, which is the middle or central part formed of cabins, chapels and sails, a throne or small constructions of one or two storeys provided with windows and a door. On the prow and the poop there were sometimes kiosks with columns in the form of a lotus flower or papyrus plant or without any decoration, supporting a raised roof.

In the tomb of Tutankhamun a complete royal flotilla and boats for every occasion were unearthed. Twenty magnificent wooden boats plastered and painted in bright colours were discovered against the eastern wall in the annex; their lengths vary from less than one to more than two and a half metres and their prows were pointing towards the east. These boats fall into two distinct categories: religious and those used for navigation on the Nile.

The tomb's boats are all of hardwood covered with a plaster coating and decorated; they constitute a complete fleet formed of the following:

- 1. A papyrus skiff for the delta floods,
- 2. Two with the prow and the poop in the shape of a papyrus turned towards the interior, for nocturnal voyages,
- 3. Four solar barques for daytime movements with prows and poops in the shape of lotus, a gilded throne for the king and rudders,
- 4. Eight rowing boats with large cabins of several storeys equipped with a door and windows and small brightly painted daises at the front and back,
- 5. Three well preserved sailing ships with sails, equipped with vast central cabins of several storeys and small daises at the front and back for the pharaoh or captain.

The boat in the tomb symbolizes several ideas, the various stages of the great annual *Opet* festival, and its seat represents the throne of the royalty of Horus, on which gods and kings believed themselves to appear to be Ra during ceremonies. The boat evokes the small papyrus barque, which the flood brought back bearing as a single passenger, the throne of which the royal personage will take possession on the day of rebirth.

The images of the boat in the tomb made it possible for the deceased to identify himself with Ra, to sail on the pond in his garden and the Nile and also allowed the soul of the deceased to traverse the night world in the solar boat, to help the deceased against the crocodile and the Apophis snake during his dangerous voyage. Chapter 99 of the Book of the Dead guarantees the deceased a boat in the kingdom of the dead, and contains a long dialogue between the ferryman and the parties in his boat

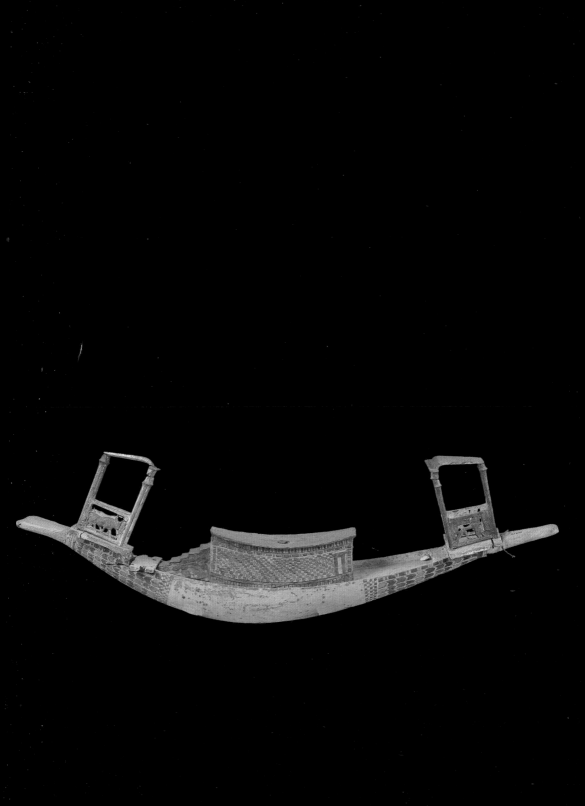

SAILING BOAT

A boat in solid wood plastered and painted, its lower part is decorated on each side with drawings of geometrical and floral themes in blue, red and yellow. It is composed of a main part, which is the central cabin formed of a construction provided with access steps and decorated in red, blue and yellow squares framed by a geometrical frieze.

A long wooden stick is fixed in the middle of the central chapel with a sail and ropes made of flax.

The front and back of the boat are called the prow and the poop; they are occupied by two kiosks in the style of the sanctuaries of Upper Egypt, which have a curved roof on one side only, supported by four columns. One of the two kiosks is decorated with a lion with a human head (sphinx) walking, preceded by the cartouche of King Nebkheperure and the other is decorated with a bull, these two representations are covered with gold leaf.

The boat is provided with a rudder placed at the prow, this is decorated at the top with a royal head wearing a conical crown surmounted by a solar disk, the head has a straight beard.

CALCITE BARQUE

Height: 37cm, width: 58. 3 cm

This masterpiece from the tomb of King Tutankhamun was found in the antechamber. It takes the form of a boat lying on a pedestal inside a rectangular tank resting on four feet; the whole made from calcite.

The tank is embellished with an Egyptian throat cornice on the upper part, a decoration very famous in ancient Egypt, followed by friezes of various types of coloured glass, square, round, khekeru (pointed floral motif) and other geometrical forms.

On the narrower sides of the tank, a square surmounted by the pet sign of the sky contains three cartouches surmounted by the nub sign of gold, two belonging to King Tutankhamun are crowned by two feathers and a solar disk, while the third with a mortar surmounted by two feathers, belongs to his wife Queen Ankhesenamun. On the right and the left are two uræi wearing the two crowns of Egypt, one with the wadjet Red Crown above the papyrus and the White Crown unusually called *neit*, surmounting the lotus; both are provided with the ankh and was sceptres.

The calcite boat is incised with blue motifs in the form of geometrical and floral patterns highlighted with gold. The prow and the poop encircled by very fine gold leaf incised with blue decorations take the form of an animal's head, probably an Asian ibex with natural horns taken from a smaller animal, and the eyes encrusted with rock crystal, and earrings hanging from its ears.

In the middle of the boat is a chapel intended for the queen, housed under a dado supported by four small columns with double lotus and papyriform capitals, these columns are also incised with red and blue and are decorated at the top, middle and bottom with fine gold leaf. The areas between the columns are finely decorated with geometrical and floral motifs in the same colours.

The queen is represented nude in a relaxed seated pose at the front of the boat, holding in her hand against her bosom, a lotus flower symbol of recreation. She is wearing a short wig with layers of curls, bracelets of fine gold on her forearms and a bracelet of pearls around her wrist.

At the other end of the boat is a standing dwarf with deformed body, and short bandy legs. She wears a short wig with a large braid, which falls to one side and has gold armlets on her forearms. This dwarf was for the queen's amusement.

Dwarves in ancient Egypt fell into two categories, locally born with natural deformities and African dwarves of pygmies brought from Africa or Punt to dance and sing in front of the tombs, which certainly had a religious significance. These dances kept the bad spirits away from the tomb, which explains the choice of a dwarf god Bes to protect the sleeping and women in childbirth. Dwarves worked in the goldsmith trade as their fingers were very deft; they personified leisure and pleasures.

A female dwarf is quite rare in representations; she served as a maidservant to the queen and at the same time accompanied her on walks and danced in the palace.

The function of this boat is not known, but the material and the fine quality of its execution give an idea of its use, it could have served as a form of lighting and at the same time push away bad spirits, by filling the empty part of the basin (the tank) with water and letting blocks of scented grease or wax containing a lighted thread, float on the surface of water.

CALCITE IBEX VASE

Length: 38.5 cm, width: 18.5 cm, height: 27.5 cm.

A calcite vase in a new form of a recumbent ibex on an oval base with its legs folded beneath it, discovered in the antechamber of the tomb; the animal is carved in an original manner by a sculptor who was undoubtedly a nature lover, a subject matter which appeared with the art of the Aten period.

The body is cut from one block of yellowish calcite except for some added parts made from other materials; the tongue is ivory stippled in red, and the horns are cut from real horn.

Traces of dark blue can be seen on the long ears, eyes, the features of the muzzle, the animal's shoes, tail and the cartouche of King Nebkheperure drawn on the side of the body, surmounted by two feathers and a solar disk.

The eyes are wide open and inlaid with clear quartz with painted details on the back, and the mouth is half-open which lets one see the tongue; the tail of the animal curves upwards. One of the horns is no longer in existence; it has either broken off or worn away.

DECORATED PERFUME VASE WITH THE NILE GOD (HAPY)

Height: 70 cm, width: 36.8 cm

Vase of calcite, ivory and gold expressing three dimensionally the concept of the unification of the two lands or *sematauy*; it was placed between the doors of the first and second of the four *naos* set around the sarcophagi and mummy of Tutankhamun, and was filled with resin and grease, perhaps to repel the bad spirits of the dead thanks to its strong odour.

The vase is made of two pieces fixed to each other; the upper part is formed of two marvellously carved images of Hapy, a full face, characterized by a heavy body, drooping chest, the rotund belly symbolizing the fertility of the earth and the benefits brought by the Nile; under their stomachs two bands of a belt slip out. They are wearing striped wigs with their respective emblems: the papyrus for the Nile of Lower Egypt and the lotus for the Nile of Upper Egypt.

The second part of the vase carries the names of Tutankhamun and his wife Queen Ankhsenamon. It is a base of which the upper part takes the form of an Egyptian throat cornice; the front and back faces have the same motif, two solar falcons surmounting the *nub* sign signifying gold, encircling a royal cartouche. On one side is the coronation name and on the other the birth name; the two cartouches each lean on a *was* sign, which means prosperity; the details are rendered in gold leaf and pieces of painted ivory.

Hapy, the god of the inundation is nearly always represented standing or walking seldom seated or kneeling; he is fat, with a characteristic hairstyle, which represents the two heraldic plants, the lotus and the papyrus, with a divine beard and a kilt knotted under the belly. He is generally provided with a table or a salver on which he brings the gifts of the Nile; he did not have a sanctuary, but was worshipped in several temples. The king and the priesthood addressed hymns to the Nile that expressed their fears and their hopes; Hapy restored life with the floodwaters.

The god here is set outside the container and is not the central artery; the two heraldic plants the lotus and the papyrus, represent the south and the north of the country. The two lands are represented by two *uraei* serpent goddesses, which surmount the vertical stems, respectively wearing the crowns of the north and the south.

The opening of the vase is sealed with bindings, but the stopper which topped the opening and was most likely of a precious substance has disappeared. It probably represented the king shielded by the protective form of Nekhbet, with wings made of ivory spread behind him.

The two lands are evoked on several occasions: on the head of Hapy, on each side of the central artery the two plants the lotus and the papyrus are tied together around the container, on two columns around which the two plants are tied behind the god Hapy, each column surmounted by a *uræus*, one wearing the White Crown, the other the red.

Although there were a great number of calcite vases containing unguents in the tomb, it is noticeable that all the vases carry the *renpet* or year sign and the number one hundred thousand according to the sign of the tadpole attached to this sign, or Heh, god of eternity followed by the *renpet* millions *of* years sign. But the vase in question does not carry either of these signs it consists only of the god of the Nile inundation. The presence of the god Hapy is the manifestation of eternity and the renewal of life each year, since the Nile rises annually, which explains the absence of the sign of the years.

HEAD OF LEOPARD

Height: 16.5 cm.

This piece is of plastered and gilded wood, it represents the head of leopard with eyes of inlaid crystal and blue glass outlining them, the muzzle, the details between the eyes and the tears, which have disappeared today, either plucked out or simply fallen and been lost. On the front, the cartouche of King Nebkheperure is engraved in various colours.

This head was fixed to a real or fake panther's skin used as a cloak by the sem priest. The king also donned this skin during festivals and ceremonies to take on the qualities, blessing and protection of the priests; he preserved these clothes in his tomb as proof of his religious role.

The priests were very important elements in the Egyptian establishment selected from among the senior officials of the court; they could read and write hieroglyphs, as well as being highly cultured having an understanding not only of theology, but also of arithmetic, astronomy, measurement, music and religious literature. The priests were charged with composing hymns and carrying out the cult celebrations in the king's name. They received the foreign tribute that the king donated to the temple or directed to the workshops of the gods.

Among the priests were those who kept the temples and cult objects clean by sprinkling them with water;, they applied makeup to the statues of the gods at the time of the processions and carried their statues or their holy barques; there were also the mortuary priests, the funerary priests, the mummification priests, the carriers of the rolls of papyrus, the priests in charge of the offerings service, the priests who announced the prescribed hour of the rituals and studied the horoscopes of the stars to determine the times of the services.

And among the names of known priests: the wer-mau priests, who were the great seers or the heads of the priesthood of Ra in Heliopolis, the hem-neter, who were the servants of the god, the it-neter, who were the fathers of the god, the wer-kherep-hemat, who were the great masters of art, the lector or wabu, who were pure in charge of looking after the instruments of worship and sacred objects, and daily worship, the khery-hebet, whose functions were to enact the ceremonies according to the ritual and to recite the sacred hymns out loud during the services, then the imiut-set-sa, probably in charge of all manual work inside the temple, and finally the sem priests, who presided over the funerals.

During the Old Kingdom the clothing of the priests were barely distinguishable from that of the people; in later times, they continued to wear the kilt and avoided the robes that came into fashion in accordance with the tastes of the day. The clothes generally worn by the priests were made of linen, which was a virgin material woven in three types, thick, medium and fine, naturally the latter was reserved for the kings, while the former was for the priests. As for the head priest, he wore a panther's skin brought from the country of Punt, adorned by our golden head decorated with a lapis lazuli tip; sometimes gold rosettes were added in emulation of the pattern on the animal's skin.

The holding of a temple service was accompanied by strict important requirements beforehand. In the morning the priests went to the temple's sacred lake to purify and wash themselves in the cold water; this operation was repeated several times a day. Another form of purification to which the priest was subjected before entering the holy place, consisted in washing out the mouth with a little natron. The priests shaved the whole body every two days, so that neither lice nor impure vermin soiled them during the exercise of worshipping. Once they had crossed the enclosure of the god and when performing their sacred duties, they were prohibited from wearing clothing made from wool, however they used a panther's skin as a sign of their dignity. Egyptian priests married but during periods in the temple, it was necessary to practice sexual abstinence.

GAMES IN ANCIENT EGYPT

The Egyptians had several kinds of games, children's toys like spinning tops made of wood, ivory or stone provided with a winding stick, wooden dolls whose limbs could be moved by means of wires. Sports included hurdling, balancing acts, shooting at a target, a game of skill, which involved throwing a pointed stick at a wooden stand, fishing, running and jumping. As for popular games, they included the game of the dog, the goose and the jackal. And finally games of contemplation, patience or chance.

Games of contemplation were much appreciated in ancient Egypt and formed part of many types of entertainment; they accompanied the deceased in his tomb together with the food offerings, because the Egyptians did not want to be deprived of this pleasure in the afterlife. These games had an entertaining role as well as a religious significance; among this type of games was one known as *senet* which means 'to pass'.

This game resembled draughts or chess and was produced in various materials and sizes. The oldest *senet* example known is made from Nile clay. The throwing pieces were in the beginning 3 x 4 = 12, but later on this was changed to 3 x 10 = 30 divided into three lines of 10 each, which explains its name "Field of 30" or "Set of 30".

The game was played everywhere and was the activity of preference during the hot summer months; it was accompanied by the text: "You sit down in the hall, you play *senet*, you have wine, you have beer". The Egyptians played it everywhere: at home, in the family and also outside in the fields, the working place and gardens.

It was played by two adversaries, its rules are known in general but the details elude us; each player received an equal number of pieces, tokens for one, bobbins for the other.

Senet dates to prehistoric times; some examples made of ivory from Abu Rauash on display in the Cairo Museum, date to the Archaic Period. During the Old Kingdom, workmen played it at the building sites of the pyramids during work breaks; Hesire, a noble of the 3rd Dynasty had a game of senet depicted on a wall of his tomb in Saqqara. Prince Ra-hotep quotes this game among the list of funerary objects in his tomb at Meidum; Mererouka of the 6th Dynasty is shown playing with his wife and her mother in a scene of his tomb. At that time, senet was played on a board made of terracotta, wood, earthenware or ivory; it was played with two pieces of two colours or two different forms decorated with the heads of a dog or a lion.

During the New Kingdom this recreational game became a funerary game of religious significance, being employed in the afterlife to distract oneself. King Ramsès III is represented on the wall of the temple of Madinet Habu playing senet with his daughters in his palace. Any, an officer played with his wife and on the wall of his tomb is a text describing senet as one of several occupations of the deceased in the afterlife. A scene of Nefertari in her tomb represents her playing senet alone.

In Chapter 17 of the Book of the Dead, the deceased player is represented in front of an often invisible adversary representing obstacles in the afterlife, or guards with the heads of fantastic animals holding knives and prohibiting the deceased's passage.

GAMING BOX ON A STAND (SENET)

Box: length: 46.6 cm, width: 14.3 cm, height: 8.1 cm.
Support: length: 55 cm, width: 17.5 cm, height: 20.2 cm.

Close to the southern wall of the annex of King Tutankhamun's tomb, four examples of the senet game were found. Each has a kind of shelf like a gaming board with thirty squares, with a drawer where the gaming pieces could be stored. This ebony specimen is an item of luxury resting on lion's legs placed within a framework, which imitates a sledge. Its box has partially gilded lion's feet on drums with ivory claws decorated with the royal titles. On its upper side it has 30 ivory squares and if the board is reversed it has 20 squares on the lower side.

The drawer that contained the playing pieces or dice was found pulled out and empty with its contents stolen, probably because the gaming pieces were made of precious materials; the pieces on the board come

from other boxes. The name of the game is drawn from the verb senet, which means 'to pass or move', while avoiding the dangerous squares on the board. It symbolized the path of death in the underworld; success against an imaginary enemy guaranteed rebirth of the deceased's spirit, provision of eternal life and joy in the underworld. As for the drawer it may indicate the afterlife, the gaming pieces were arranged in it and each time the player wanted to play a game he had to remove them, which brings to mind the sky, which creates the solar disk to swallow it again each night. The lucky player was declared maat kheru, which means justified thus benefiting from the rites, which gave him back his senses and the breath of life.

This game seems to have played an important role in the relationship between the living and the dead; he had to bypass the traps and in spite of adversary, continue on to victory.

THE BEDS

After his death the deceased required a complete set of furnishings similar to those he had used during his life on earth made up of chests, stools, chairs and beds. Eight beds were found in the tomb of Tutankhamen, three funerary, four day-to-day beds and an Osiris bed.

The four everyday beds are of a conventional appearance but they do not lack in ingenuity. They are small and their accessories come from the antechamber and the tomb's annex. They had a functional role and are identical to those discovered in the richest Egyptian residences.

All were built following the same design comprising a wooden frame surrounding a lattice composed of papyrus stems, lower at the foot than the head to ensure good circulation of the blood whilst sleeping, four lion's leg posts on drums joined by wooden batons to stabilize the bed's legs.

FOLDING BED

It is the forerunner of our modern camping bed and the only one found in Egypt. It is made from light sycamore wood and was discovered in the antechamber of the tomb of King Tutankhamun. Its dimensions are smaller as it served the king during his travels. This bed is composed of three parts joined together by heavy copper hinges; in the centre, two additional feline shaped legs are also joined by hinges, these bend back folding the bed into the shape of the letter Z.

This bed is lower than the others; its lattice is made of papyrus stems covered with a layer of plaster. The footboard is simple and has no ornamentation or decoration; the three panels are divided by two papyrus flowers, one above the other.

FUNERARY BEDS

In the antechamber of Tutankhamen's tomb three funerary beds made of plastered and gilded or painted wood and bronze, were found in the shape of sacred animals. They were standing in a row facing north towards the tomb's entrance. They are in a good state of preservation, rendered splendid by the brilliance of their gilding. They are raised and rest on solid rectangular bases. Similar beds are represented on the walls of other tombs in the Valley of the Kings, such as those of Ramses III and Seti II, where outlines of three similar to these can be seen, and fragments of these have been found in previously robbed tombs.

The sun is the being, which does not die in the evening but only sleeps and at dawn is resurrected or reborn, and these beds represent protection during this period. Their role was very important in the afterlife; the dead king was laid on one or other of these in order to be reanimated according to the three phases of resurrection. The beds would carry him to his eternal residence; at the top of each an inscription of Osiris-Nebkheperure confirms the role they played for the late king.

he beds were made in identical fashion and consisted of four elements, a base whose surface imitated a plaited rug, a board at the end of the bed and two cross-pieces in the shape of animals within a rectangular framework, joined together by hooks, rings and squares made of a copper alloy. They were dismounted to be transported to the museum and clear indications of their reassembly can be seen on the necks of the animals. The beds varied in size and were arranged from the smallest to the largest when they were found in the antechamber.

The base was plastered and gilded then laid on boards made from plant stems. The footboard with the two ends supported on both sides, carried a strictly funerary decoration in light relief composed of two pairs of the back part of the *djed* pillar of Osiris, symbol of stability, framing two *tyet* knots of the belt of Isis, symbol of eternity.

FUNERARY BED REPRESENTING MEKHIT (LIONESS)

Length: 180 cm, width: 91cm, height: 156 cm.

The first bed is in the shape of a lioness and according to the text registered across the top, is identified with Mekhit (a form of Hathor, Sekhmet and Isis). She is the distant goddess who returns appeased to bring the Nile floods from which the country lives; the bent tails of the lions frame a block decorated with *djed* pillars and *tyet* knots. The features are admirably emphasized with the nose inlaid in blue glass, and the tears of clear quartz running from the eyes outlined in black, while the retina is of painted crystal.

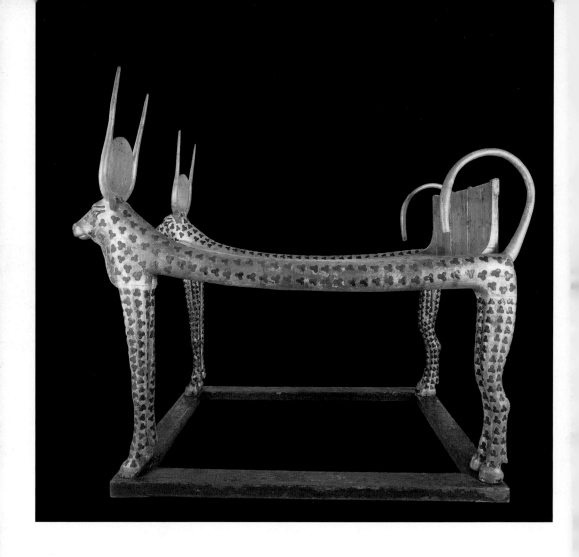

FUNERARY BED REPRESENTING ISIS-MEHIT (COW)

Length: 208 cm, width: 128 cm, height: 188 cm.

The second bed is more elongated and slightly lower than the first. Two long legged cows constitute the longer sides of this bed. Their bodies are inlaid with three-pointed blue glass spots, the base of the tails is emphasized by red paint and the splendid horns encircle a flattened image of the sun. The panel of the footboard is decorated with the *djed* pillar and *tyet* knot, flanked by the two arched tails of the animals, which form almost a complete circle. The eyes are of clear quartz with painted details, the facial features are coloured and the eyebrows are of blue glass.

This goddess is often associated with Isis, she was the primordial cow, which emerged from the waters of the primordial sea *nwn* and carried the sun god Rā to the horizon of the sky. She is represented on the walls of Theban burial chambers in the form of a crouching cow or one which is rearing proudly.

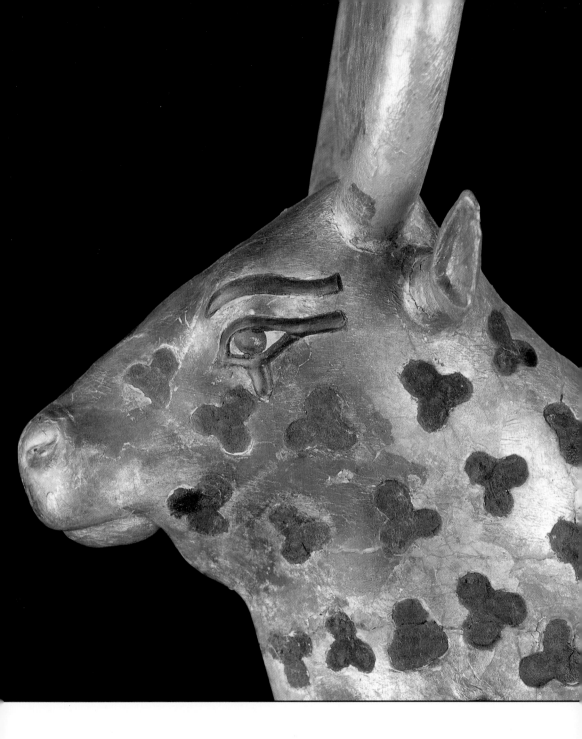

FUNERARY BED REPRESENTING AMMUT (HIPPOPOTAMUS)

Length: 236 cm, width: 126 cm, height: 134 cm.

The third bed is unusually longer than the other two but is narrower and lower; it carries the representation of the composite goddess Ammut, (the large devourer) that which devours death, as the inscription between the two heads informs us. She appears in the scenes of the weighing of the heart during the judgment of Osiris, (scene of psycho-ecstasy) to devour the hearts of those who do not receive permission to enter the kingdom of Osiris.

Ammut is a composite goddess with the head of a hippopotamus, the body of a crocodile and the legs of a lion. The tails are different this time, being short and tapering not curved, and between the two is a tripartite panel with the same decoration: the *djed* and *tyet* signs. The mouth is open with the tongue and teeth made of ivory, dyed red for the former; the details of the eyes are painted in black and white with traces of red, to give more vivacity to the animal.

THE CHESTS

As the tomb was the eternal house of the king, it had to contain all that he will need from his terrestrial life. More than fifty chests and boxes of various dimensions were discovered in the tomb of Tutankhamun, some contained precious objects but were found open and empty. There is nothing primitive about their design, technique and method of manufacture, they could be used nowadays.

Their main component is wood but sometimes of very modest quality, however, enriched with inlays, gilding, glass and semi-precious and precious materials, and ivory and ebony marquetry.

These chests were used as drawers or wall cupboards into which were put clothes, sandals, jewels, perfume pots, makeup tools or musical instruments, mirrors, combs, oils and even the canopic vases and papyri.

The chests generally follow a simple plan being made in wood and provided with handles, which are fixed to the body and the lid, a rope holds the two handles together to facilitate closing the chest.

They also can differ on some points like the dimensions, shape, lid, and decoration. Some are small enough to be carried by one or two workers, while others are of a considerable size necessitating several servants. The chests can be rectangular, square, cylindrical or arch shaped. As for the lid, it is sometimes triangular and pointed, or rounded on only one side like the roof of a chapel in Upper Egypt, or rounded in the middle and framed by two vertical posts like the roof of a chapel of Lower Egypt, or simply flat. The chests are sometimes resting on small feet decorated with a pattern called throat cornice, which is repeated on the upper part of the body.

Egyptian wood is of moderate quality and local species like sycamore, acacia, palm tree and tamarix were useful for manufacturing chests and small statues, but ebony and cedar that were woods imported in antiquity from Punt and of Phoenicia, were used for the manufacture of the sarcophagi, flag staffs, coffins and royal furniture.

CHEST WITH PAINTED DECORATION

Length: 61 cm, width: 43 cm, Height 44,5 cm

One of the most outstanding objects in the collection of Tutankhamun. A splendid chest, considered one of the museum's major pieces and a magnificent example of perfect preservation. It is of plastered wood painted with an extraordinary finesse; it was found in the antechamber of the tomb and was used to protect several objects found inside: a pair of papyrus sandals, three pairs of gold sandals, a gilded headrest, robes trimmed with pearls, scarves, necklaces and a tiger's skin.

The chest is decorated with the symmetrical parallel scenes of war traditionally represented on the fronts of temples and pylons during the New Kingdom; the scenes are bordered by a geometrical floral framework with inlays of coloured glass and semi-precious materials.

The two main sides decorated with military scenes are surmounted by a *ret* sign, symbol of the sky, which represented the king's authority over the void that separates the sky from the earth, under which is drawn a solar disk flanked by two *uraei* each holding the *ankh* sign of life and offering it to the king.

To the right and left of the disk are two images of the vulture goddess Nekhbet with the *chen* sign in their claws to ensure eternity for the king; they are protecting the whole scene and give the breath of life to the king by spreading their wings close to his nose.

The representation of the king standing in his chariot pulled by two harnessed horses with feathers on their heads, and launching into a gallop, divides the scene into two different parts: the enemies and the Egyptian army.

The king is wearing a short kilt and a corselet of panther's skin tied at the chest, he is drawing a bow, while his chariot is crushing his enemies; he is wearing the blue *khepresh* war crown and is attacking his enemies; on one side of the chest are Syrians, northern enemies and on the other Nubians, enemies from the south. The difference between the two is clear from the colour of the skin, style of the hair, beards, clothes and facial features.

Behind the king, three fan bearers are protecting him; they are followed by the Egyptian army divided into three working parties placed in three rows. Two in chariots and a third on foot, they are very well organized, calm and are surrounded by plants and shrubs, which are symbols of peace.

On the left it is completely the reverse, the enemies are in disorder and confusion; the artist has depicted the smallest details of the facial features, bows, arrows, shields and the horses, very well. At the bottom of the scene, the king is setting his dogs to attack and is trampling the enemy; it is a complete victory for the king.

The two narrower sides represent almost identical scenes, surrounded by friezes of a check pattern and stylized flowerets. Each side is surmounted by a winged solar disk, which protects one of the king's cartouches surrounded by two *uræi*. The centre of the scene is occupied by two of the king's cartouches, side by side, which are placed on the *nub* sign of gold surmounted by two feathers and a solar disk.

To the right and left of the two cartouches, two sphinxes are depicted, on one side wearing a wig and the composite *atef* crown of Osiris made up of a cone, two feathers, two horns and the *uræus* at the front, and on the other side with the *nemes* or the royal striped headdress. The sphinxes are trampling on the traditional enemies, a Nubian, a Libyan and an Asian.

The lid is arched and made from two pieces separated by a central band of hieroglyphics. Each side depicts a hunting scene surrounded by friezes of a check pattern and rosettes. On the first side of the lid, the king is shown standing in his chariot with his bow and shooting his arrows at wild animals, lions and lionesses, tigers and hyenas, while the king's dog is attacking the wounded animals.

On the other side there is another hunting scene, but this time, the king is hunting game animals like antelopes, a couple of ostriches and wild asses. These two scenes represent the king's victory and are in contrast to the two battles on the main body of the chest.

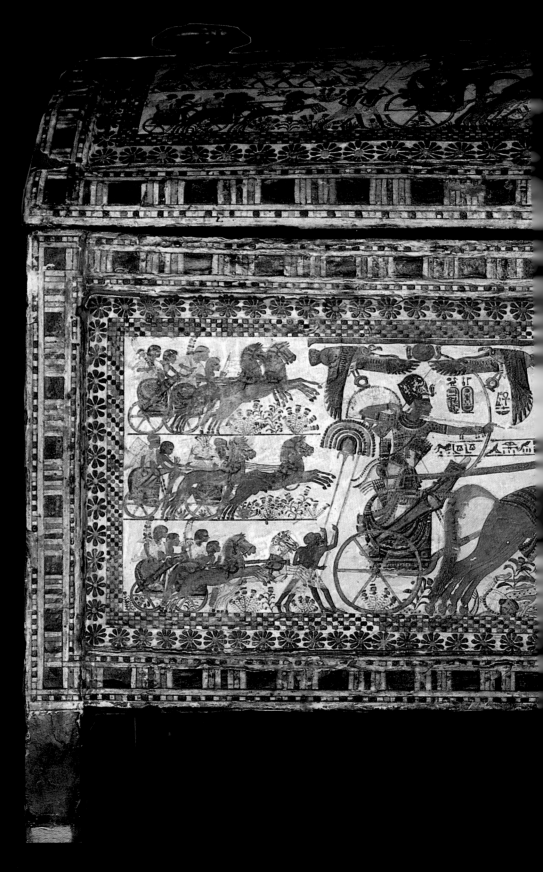

VENEERED IVORY CHEST

Width: 40.6 cm, Height: 63.5 cm.

This chest counts as one of most beautiful of Tutankhamun; it was found in the tomb's antechamber, overturned and emptied by robbers who had ransacked the burial in antiquity, with its lid thrown into a corner. The chest was probably intended to contain the valuable robes of the king such as the ceremonial dress, which bore almost the same symbols.

It is a rectangular ebony chest veneered with painted ivory, inlaid with glass, bronze and gold; it is in a perfect state of preservation and owes its inspiration to the architectural detail of a gold plated Egyptian throat cornice; the rounded top forms the lid. The trunk is elevated on legs with bronze feet, which extend upwards to form a single post; as usual two gilded knobs form the closing system.

The scenes meet two essential requirements, the relationship of a couple in love and the pleasures of hunting in the marshes. The trunk's decoration consists of a geometrical framework and a luxuriant verdant landscape, where either the royal couple or a frieze of animals appears. As for the decoration of the lid this contains the principal scene, which represents the centre of this dream world.

The scene is bordered by two friezes: one is geometrical and the other floral made up of bunches of several kinds of flowers, since the scene is that of a marriage in a garden. The standing figures of the king and queen are clearly seen, they are richly dressed and wearing their jewellery.

The queen conveys all the elements of temptation, she is a royal wife at the height of her beauty: A sumptuous headdress, a cone of scented oil flanked by two solar *uræi* and two disks are posed on her wig, from which escapes a heavy thick braid decorated with jewels.

She has a *uræus* on her forehead and there are two large earrings between her hair and the ornamental collar around her neck. Her white pleated dress tied with a yellow ribbon, which falls to her sandals, reveals the details of her well rounded body. The queen is offering the king two large bouquets of papyrus and lily mixed with mandrake, the fruits of love and seduction.

The well dressed king is also wearing an ornamental collar around his throat, hiding his shoulders and chest. He is wearing a charming wig of locks from which the ribbons float behind his back, a pleated kilt with a broad belt, which falls to the knees, and sandals on his feet. He is leaning on a cane with one hand, and is extending the other in a pleasing gesture to receive the bouquets from the queen. In the lower part of the scene, two kneeling servants are gathering mandrake and making bouquets.

On the main body of the chest there are two important scenes, a small hunting one and another of fishing, which show Tutankhamun comfortably seated on a decorated cushion on a seat with floral ornamentation, while his wife, the queen sits at his feet. He is in front of a small lake in a garden and is aiming at the birds and fish.

The king is wearing the blue *khepresh* crown of war from which two ribbons are suspended, his ears have pierced lobes, he is wearing an ornamental collar, a double length pleated kilt and a belt, and sandals, and is standing on a pedestal.

Tutankhamun is shooting arrows at the wild ducks, which populate the papyrus thickets while at the same time he is fishing in a pool filled with fish. One arrow passes behind the king's neck to ensure it does not cut his body, while another has just hit one of the water birds flying over the pond, which is filled with large fish.

Queen Ankhsenpaton in an official position of accompanying and helping her husband, is squatting on a cushion at his feet, turning her head towards him and holding an arrow in her left hand ready to pass to him, and in her right hand is a lotus flower symbol of peace and recreation. She is wearing a pleated dress tied with a belt, a short wig held in place by a headband and surmounted by a perfumed cone. A servant with a bent back is gathering the fish and fowl caught and shot by the king.

This operation is symbolic, when the king kills the fish and the ducks, he is killing evil. These two creatures are symbols of evil as are the hippopotamuses, snakes, crocodiles, asses and tortoises.

On three sides of the chest, painted panels show animals being hunted not only by the king but also by other hunters.

On the longer sides, a spotted calf is rising to its feet; an ibex in flight is being attacked by the king's lion, taken together with the dogs and the lions all depicting great freedom of movement. A Syrian ibex is being bitten by a dog with a collar around its neck, a spotted bull is being attacked by a cheetah, which has jumped on its back, a spotted calf is being bitten by a dog and an ibex is fleeing.

DECORATED CHEST IN THE SHAPE OF THE GOD HEH

This gilded wooden chest richly decorated with blue faience inlays was found in the antechamber. It is made up of a body and lid, each of which has two blue faience knobs decorated with the two cartouches of King Tutankhamun.

The lid is curved like roofs of the chapels in Upper Egypt. The two lateral sides carry the image of a winged serpent whose body forms successive curves and in front of this is engraved the *ankh* sign of life. An Egyptian throat cornice runs around the body of the chest.

The two longer sides of the chest have identical scenes bordered by a geometrical pattern of squares inlaid in brown and blue glass; the scene consists of the repetition of the two cartouches of King Tutankhamun, each encircled by two *uræi* wearing gilded solar disks.

The shorter sides are occupied by a frame containing two representations of Heh, god of eternity, a human god, his head surmounted by a gilded solar disk and his two raised hands holding the *renpet* sign of the years, to which are added the *chen* and the tadpole symbol of a hundred thousand years.

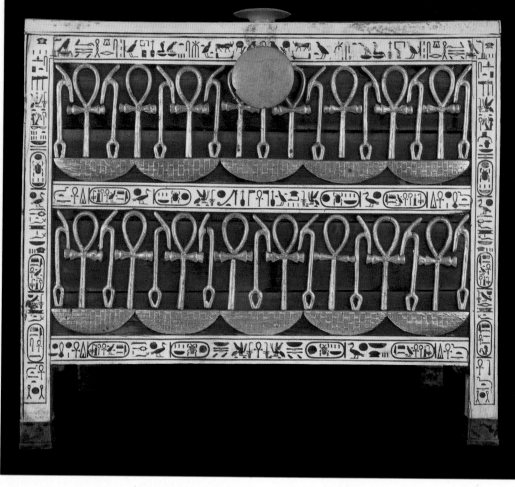

CHEST WITH OPENWORK DECORATION

Height: 42.5 cm, length: 8.2 cm, width: 44.4 cm.

This chest in a very good state of preservation is of simple design, but fashioned in a very high quality and elegant manner; it has four feet and a flat lid. It is made from a light wood enriched by ivory and gilded wood marquetry; it was pillaged by robbers and then hastily repacked.

It comprises sixteen internal compartments intended to contain the king's valuable objects, which had disappeared at the time of its discovery, but with the writing instruments still intact.

The decoration comprises four hieroglyphic signs, two *was* signs (prosperity) surrounding an *ankh* sign (life) in the middle, and the three placed on the *neb* sign (all); this motif is repeated on all sides of the chest and the lid as well.

The feet of the chest have bronze fittings and the knobs are of pink tinted ivory. On the ivory frieze, which goes round the whole body of the chest, are texts composed of the **titles** and epithets of the king, in addition to the name of Queen Ankhsenamon.

JEWELLERY

Jewellery during prehistoric times consisted of shell and clay beads, but during historical times it became of great beauty and of a considerable variety. The Old Kingdom produced many jewels manufactured of gold inset with ivory or precious stones. With the Middle Kingdom the art of the goldsmith attained perfection in its finesse and elegance. The pre-eminence of the New Kingdom was expressed by the great richness of its jewellery.

The collars are of enamel or glass beads or semi-precious stones: lapis lazuli, jasper, cornelian and feldspar. They are composed of one or more rows of gold beads; the collar was offered to divinities like Amun and the gift of a collar from a pharaoh was a great reward.

The bracelets were of gold, silver, bronze, ivory, enamel or they consisted of stone beads mounted on a gold wire.

The rings, which decorated one or more fingers, were worked in all metals even iron, enamel and quartz. Earrings appeared with the New Kingdom; they were generally worn by women and were engraved in gold in the shapes of a crescent moon, flowers, large circles, and fans.

With gold, the goldsmith engraved precious objects with geometrical shapes imitating butterflies and flowers. They also fashioned amulets representing the gods or sacred animals and pectorals, which were heavy pieces of royal jewellery worn on the chest, formed of a rectangle enclosing figurative representations in fine stones and engraved gold.

And in spite of the abundance of jewellery discovered in the tomb of Tutankhamun, it is thought that it does not represent the total of the variety at the disposal of a sovereign of the 18th Dynasty. The jewellery discovered between the strips of the mummy and in the chests in the tomb, fulfilled funerary and religious functions. Thieves undoubtedly seized the pharaoh's personal jewellery, they were certainly extraordinary in the choice of materials and the techniques employed.

The objects found in the tomb are not identical and testify to the various techniques employed by the artists who were able to work gold, to create pieces of gold wire holding inlays, to make drawings, and to produce inlays in enamel and glass paste.

PECTORAL WITH THE SUN RISING ON THE HORIZON

Length of necklace: 50 cm, width of pectoral: 11.8 cm.

This extremely beautiful pectoral is a masterpiece of the Cairo Museum; it was discovered in the wooden box inlaid with ivory and gold. This pectoral depicts the myth of the sun in an ambiance of richness, delicacy and elegance.

The skill of the goldsmiths who worked on this piece is only equalled by the quality of the inlays of lapis lazuli, turquoise, cornelian and feldspar, some of the beads are of coloured glass paste. The collar also contains gold plaques, which give it value and lustre. The use of gold here is essential, since the pectoral conveys the idea of the myth of the rising sun as an object of worship.

The weak point of the pectoral is the modest choice of two rows of red, blue and green glass paste beads; this was for practical reasons.

The centre of the pectoral is defined by a large blue scarab with the body details defined in gold wire. Its top and bottom ends each rest on a surface made up of four rows of coloured glass paste and gold beads.

The scarab is Khepery, the insect, which represents the sun at dawn, posed on the solar boat made of solid shining gold. This scarab is flanked by two pillars decorated with the *nefer*, *ankh* and *djed*, the symbolic amulets of beauty, life and stability; these amulets are inlaid with turquoise, lapis lazuli and cornelian. The two pillars flanking the scarab are bordered by two large *uræi* surmounted by a cornelian solar disk encircled in gold, they are attached by a gold wire at the boat's two curved ends.

The scarab has the habit of emerging from the sand pushing a ball of excrement before him, but here this ball is replaced by the cornelian solar disk encircled with gold and bordered by two *uræi* inlaid with semi-precious stones.

The two long bands of the pectoral are identical and end in the counterweight attached to the collar. These bands take the form of a motif, which is repeated twice. It is composed of a blue scarab posed on the *sed* sign meaning jubilee, surmounted by a gilded solar disk flanked by two *uræi* separated by the *ankh* sign of life. To these is added the motif of a double *djed* pillar, symbol of stability, resting on the *sed* jubilee sign, surmounted by a solar disk of cornelian encircled in gold.

The upper parts of the two bands are curved towards the interior, forming the shapes of the bodies of two vultures with folded wings looking towards each other, personifying Nekhbet the protective goddess of the pharaoh of Upper Egypt. The two vultures are inlaid with coloured glass paste.

The counterweight is attached to the collar by four rows of gold wire and beads. At the same time this forms the collar's clasp; it is composed of two *uræi* placed side by side inlaid with semi-precious materials, and separated by a element in solid gold, which is used to open the collar

This pectoral very clearly depicts the sun rising at dawn, which symbolizes rebirth and the eternal life forecast for the king. The scarab is the star that appears on his boat in the morning accompanied by the wish for life, beauty and stability under the protection of the divinities Nekhbet and Wadjet, which are repeated several times.

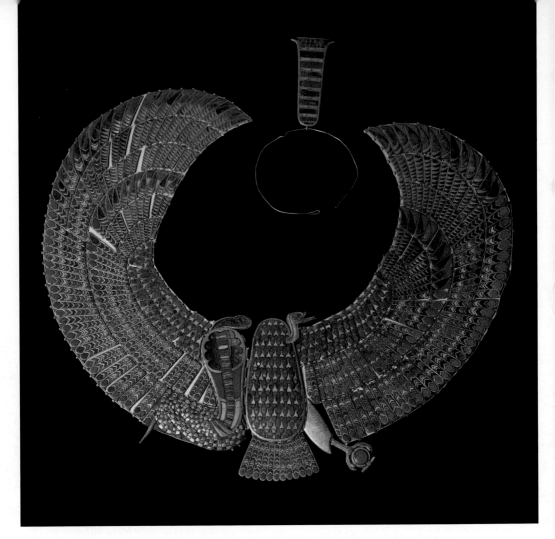

PECTORAL OF THE TWO LADIES: NEKHBET AND WADJET

Width: 48.7 cm

A beautiful and very stylish large pectoral discovered with two others in the chest area between the strips of King Tutankhamun's mummy. This piece is known by the name of (The pectoral of the two ladies), the *uræus* Wadjet and the vulture Nekhbet (the Nebti), the two divinities, who protected the pharaoh as the sovereign of Upper and Lower Egypt. Similar pectorals are represented on the lids of wooden sarcophagi dating to the Middle Kingdom.

The two divinities are represented in an unusual way as they are joined together by two large wings, which connect them. The *uræus* is coiled back on itself, its body taking the form of a pattern of squares, which end in a pointed gold tail. The vulture has only one leg whose claws are holding a *shen* sign, symbol of eternity. The two very beautiful goddesses are inlaid with glass paste coloured red, turquoise blue and dark blue. The head of the vulture is moulded and worked in gold, the details are engraved and the beak is of obsidian. The snake's body is represented by alternating inlays of gold and glass paste.

This pectoral is flexible and perfectly established on an irregular base. Without taking into account the bodies of the two goddesses, it is composed of 171 gold plaques joined together by small eyelets placed at the top and bottom extremities of each; a fine silver wire passes between the eyelets and holds the plaques together. The back of the plaques is engraved with a feather motif, as for the front it has a cloisonné pattern and is inlaid with coloured glass paste, cut to fit the shape of each section.

At the two ends of the pectoral, a more intense use of gold and the gradual disappearance of colour is noticeable, whilst retaining the red coloured inlay for the tips.

This pectoral like the others has a counterweight at the back to hold it in place; the counterweight resembles a bell in shape and is made of gold with inlays of coloured glass paste. It is connected to the pectoral by a gold wire fixed to the back.

PECTORAL NECKLACE WITH THREE SCARABS

Width of pectoral: 9 cm, width of counterweight: 5.3 cm, length of collar: 18.5 cm.

This necklace was placed around the neck of the king and although it is a sombre piece, it bears many important symbols. The principal decoration consists of three blue lapis lazuli scarabs each signifying existence. They are placed side by side and are connected by gold fasteners, with a *neb* basket, the sign meaning (all) inlaid with green feldspar above them.

The scarabs are surmounted by a single *pet* or sign of the sky made of gold, and a disk is posed on each of these scarabs. The one in the middle made from electrum is the lunar disk surmounting a lunar crescent, but the two disks on both sides are of gold and represent the solar disk.

The grouping of these symbols presents the idea of the name of King Tutankhamun, the *neb* basket sign and the tripling of the scarabs represent the plural sign used in writing Kheperu, the name of the sovereign in addition to the solar disk. Therefore, we have the name Nebkheperure under the protection of the sun and the moon, symbolizing day and night and thus birth and death.

Beneath the scarabs is a horizontal band composed of 12 flowers of coloured glass paste and gold. From this band are suspended four lotus flowers interspersed with three large buds of the same flower. The inlays of the flowers and buds are of cornelian, feldspar and blue glass paste.

Five rows of cylindrical-shaped gold beads appear from the two gilded disks at the ends. These are separated by small coloured glass paste beads forming two long strips, which are the two sides of the necklace connecting the pectoral to the counterweight. They are held in place by solid gold clasps, engraved and decorated with long winged, coiled *uræi*.

The counterweight is beautiful: it is composed of a man kneeling on a band divided into several squares inlaid with blue and red glass paste. His figure is inlaid with ivory and feldspar and he is raising his arms thus resembling Shu, god of the air. This god usually supports the sky, but here he is holding in his hands a long cartouche engraved with the king's forename, title and epithet: (The beneficial god Nebkheperure chosen of Amun-Ra), this cartouche replaces the sky between Shu's hands.

The divinity also resembles Heh god of a million years or eternity, symbolizing the desire of a million years for the sovereign, but the *renpet* sign meaning year, is missing from his emblems.

The god resting his right arm on the *uræus* is surmounted by the White Crown, symbol of Upper Egypt fashioned in gold and inlaid with coloured glass paste. As for his left hand, it is resting on the *djed* pillar and *was* sign, symbolizing stability and prosperity.

The symbolism of this pectoral is very clear from the grouping of some elements: King Nebkheperure (three beetles on the basket occupying the pectoral), (the crescent and lunar disk) meaning death, (the sun) promising rebirth, (the god Heh) eternity, (the *was* sceptre) prosperity, (the *djed* sign) stability and (Nekhbet) power, under the protection of the symbol of recreation (the lotus), which drives out bad spirits. The whole cartouche is made lighter by the presence in gold of the important names of the two divinities Ra and Amun.

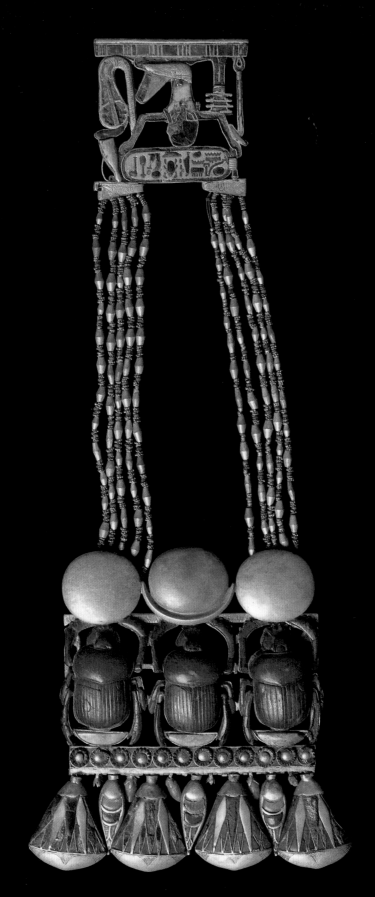

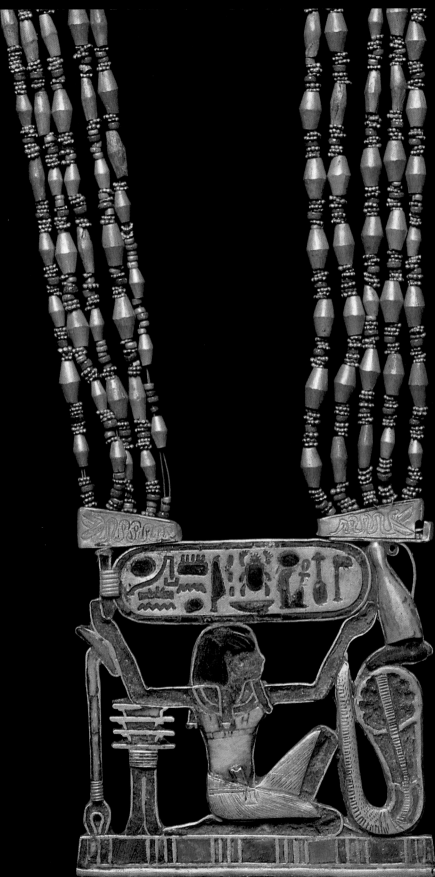

NECKLACE DECORATED WITH A WADJET EYE

Pendent height: 5.7 cm, width: 9.5 cm, length of chain: 33 cm.

This necklace was probably worn by King Tutankhamun during his lifetime because it shows traces of wear. The pendant is of solid gold with a large amount of cloisonné work. It is composed of a *wadjet* eye one of the most important amulets in Egypt, meaning perfection and health, inlaid with crystalline limestone and lapis lazuli.

The eye is flanked by the two protective goddesses Nekhbet and Wadjet. Nekhbet the vulture of Upper Egypt is wearing the White sectioned Crown with two feathers curved at the ends, carrying the *shen* sign in her claws and spreading her wings around the eyelet, and Wadjet the cobra of Lower Egypt, is wearing the Red Crown and looking in the same direction as the vulture. The inlays are of coloured glass paste, cornelian and lapis lazuli.

The pectoral is posed on a base of glass paste squares divided by gold. The counterweight composed of two *djed* and one *tyt* signs and inlaid with lapis lazuli, cornelian and glass paste, is joined to the pectoral by three rows of small beads in multicoloured glass paste with small gold pins.

EARRINGS WITH GRANULATION

Length: 10 cm.

A type of earring testifying to foreign influence most probably Nubian, commonly worn but distinguished by granulation of the gold, which was a process used throughout Egyptian history. It consisted of bringing an alloy into contact with a surface by passing it through a screen to fuse the gold into small grains. The granules were probably created by using gold dust stabilised by welding, but it is not known exactly how and which techniques were used by the Egyptian craftsmen to obtain this perfect result.

This example is formed of a gold ring from which circles of gold beads and black resin are hanging. Each bead varies in size from the inside to the outside, forming a harmonious circle. Beneath the bead circles is a rectangular element attached by three eyelets and decorated with granulated spirals, to which seven rows of gold and glass paste beads are connected by very fine gold wire. They are completed by solid gold lotus seed-shaped beads and others in the shape of drops.

The ring is decorated with stylized granulated lotus flowers and buds bound by the stems, the circles contain resin and gold beads separated by resin disks supported by fine gold circles. The gold beads are decorated with a motif of triangles and small gold bosses encircled by granules.

The method of closure is composed of a vertical bar passed through the pierced lobe and inserted into a hollow tube. The two ends are concealed by circular studs decorated with rosettes of gold wire as well as petals covered in gold leaf. The use of red gold obtained by the addition of sulphated iron is noticeable in this piece of jewellery.

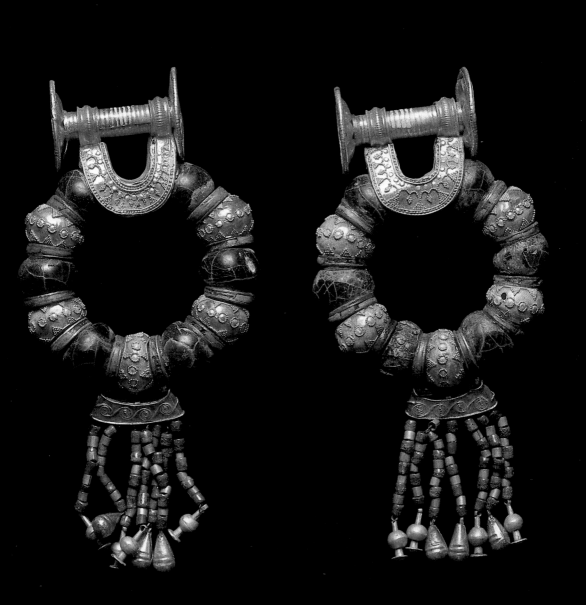

EARRINGS DECORATED WITH DUCK HEADS

Length: 10.9 cm.

These earrings were discovered in the interior of the cartouche-shaped chest in the treasury. They were worn by Tutankhamun during his childhood, put to one side at the time of puberty and then included in his funerary equipment.

This is a beautiful pair of earrings characterized by cloisonné work and other techniques. The closure is the same as for the majority of earrings, consisting of a vertical element which passes through the pierced lobe and fits into a hollow tube. An added element here is in the form of two clear quartz disks placed at the ends of the closure and decorated with two *uræi*. The semicircular closure hangs down and forms part of the earring's principal element, which has the delicate shape of a bird viewed from the front with the curved spread wings forming a complete circle. The bird's legs are also facing to the front and they hold in their claws *shen* signs, meaning eternity. The small sections of cloisonné are inlaid with quartz, calcite, faience and glass paste. The head of a bird in profile appears in the centre of the inner circle, it is not a falcon or a vulture, but a duck in a rarely used translucent blue glass paste.

The bird's tail is nicely decorated, it is edged at its extremities by a gold frieze of small disks and a border from which fringes of gilded and blue beads are suspended. The whole ends in five *uræi* represented from the front.

196

EARRINGS REPRESENTING THE PHARAOH

Length: 11.8 cm.

Earrings of spectacular appearance manufactured from poor quality gold, with inlays of various materials such as lapis lazuli, coloured glass paste and cornelian.

The closure system is the same as for the majority of the earrings. It is decorated with pieces of gold covered with some inlays of coloured glass paste, as well as *uræi*, one of which is missing, surmounted by solar disks.

The central part of each earring is formed of a gold ring, connected to the closure by a falcon with spread wings, it is made of gold inlaid with clear quartz.

The gold ring is surrounded by a granulated pattern, the whole is encircled by lenticular-shaped gold and glass paste beads. In the middle of each ring, a group formed of the king flanked by two large *uræi* surmounted by gold solar disks, is represented. The statuette of the pharaoh is of clear red cornelian, it depicts him standing and wearing the *khepresh* crown of war and a frontal *uræus*, holding the *heka* crook in his hand, the group is standing on the *heb* sign meaning festival.

From the lower part of the ring, hang rows of cornelian and green and blue glass beads, assembled in pairs and separated from each other by small gold granules. The end is formed of gold, cornelian and glass beads in the shape of drops.

GOLD BUCKLE REPRESENTING THE PHARAOH AND HIS WIFE

Length: 9 cm.

This plate is called a buckle although there is no proof attesting to this being its function, it is more correct to regard it as an attachment for a belt or clothing. Four openwork plates of the same type were judged at first to be decorative elements of chariots. They were found in a chest in the antechamber, to which three others were added whose precise location was not known.

This plate is very elaborate, it has repoussé work with engraved details and granulated additions. The gold used is red in colour as in several other pieces of funerary equipment.

The plate represents a royal kiosk crowned by two friezes, the first is a frieze made up of large *uræi* surmounted by solar disks and the second is the Egyptian cornice. The whole is surmounted by a winged solar disk between two *uræi*, two narrow incised pillars stand on the right and left.

The central scene shows Tutankhamun with his wife Queen Ankhsenamun in front of him. The king is sitting on a throne with a high back without armrests, he is resting his right arm on the seat of the throne while the other is placed on his knee. The lion-headed feet of the throne are separated by the *sematawy* decoration of the unification of Egypt, and are partly hidden by the bands falling from the king's belt. His name Nebkheperure is written in a cartouche in front of his face.

The king is wearing the *atef* crown made of feathers, a solar disk confined within two horns and two uræi surmounted by solar disks on his head, and on the forehead a fabric ribbon attached to a short smooth wig.

He is also wearing a collar on his chest with three large solar disks; the king's robe pleated with short sleeves, typical of the Amarna period, is tied under the chest letting us see the swollen belly, it finishes at the level of the feet, which are resting on a pedestal.

The queen is standing in front of the sovereign, she is the same size as him although he is seated. She is leaning slightly forward and offering him a stem of papyrus with her left hand, while tenderly stroking him with her right.

She is wearing a mortar surmounted by five feathers and three solar disks on her head. Her wig is short and smooth and attached to her forehead by a ribbon, which hangs down the nape of her neck and back, she is wearing a round gilded earring. The queen is garbed in a long, pleated transparent dress, flared and attached under the chest, ending at the level of her feet.

Behind the backs of the king and queen, two floral columns with several kinds of flowers are placed next to lateral pillars. Beneath the couple's feet, two enemies: an Asian and a Nubian bound and submissive are prone on the ground.

On the two ends of the plaque is a repetitious scene: a sphinx with the body of a lion and the head and arms of a human is lying down, it has the facial features of the king and a straight beard. On its head, it is wearing the royal (*nemes*) headdress, which finishes at the back in a kind of braid. At the top of the *nemes*, a solar disk is placed, it is bordered by two *uræi* at the side and a frontal *uræus*.

The sphinx is raising its two arms to face level and holding the *maat* sign of justice, formed by a goddess sitting on top of a basket, wearing a feather on her head and with an *ankh* sign on her knee. Behind the sphinx, a vulture holds a *shen* sign and a feather in its claws and is spreading its wings to offer protection to the king. Each element in this scene has a significance, the basket is the word (all), *maat* is justice, *ankh* is life, *shen* is eternity, thus this scene conveys the idea: (Life, protection, eternity and justice) offered to the king and his wife, who are in the centre of the plate. The decoration of this plaque is composed of a fine collar formed of small round beads side by side, which pass across the two representations of the king and queen, between the feathers of the crown, around the solar disk, above the heads of the royal couple, around their necks, waists, hips, arms and over their robes.

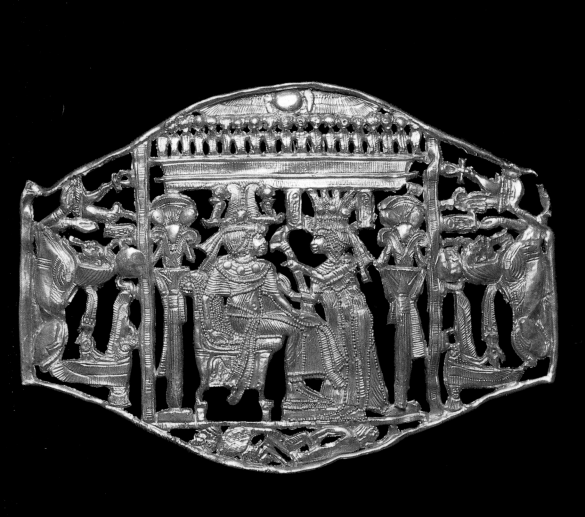

PLAQUE OF THE PHARAOH ON HIS CHARIOT

Height: 6.2 cm, width: 8.5 cm.

It is not known where this plaque of red gold was found. The principal scene represents the return from a triumphant military campaign. King Tutankhamun is depicted standing perfectly balanced on his war chariot.

The scene is surmounted by the representation of a vulture with an incised body spreading its wings and looking towards the king. Between its claws hangs the *ankh* sign symbolizing life and at the side another sign *dw* is posed, it is the sign which says: (that he is promised …). The sentence means (that he is promised life). part of the chest. The king's robe with short sleeves is transparent and pleated, and tied with two belts, one at the chest and another beneath the stomach.

The king is holding the reins, which are attached to a gilded solar disk placed close to the necks of the two galloping horses. These horses are admirably decorated with feathers and solar disks posed on their heads, and pieces of fabric with granulated decorations, their tails are long and are well combed. On the chariot, the king had arranged the quivers and arrows. Between the legs of the horses the king's dog runs quickly, it is wearing a collar around its neck.

Two prisoners, a Nubian and an Asian precede the chariot, they are standing, bound together by plant stems and wear long robes, which are engraved. Behind the chariot, the cartouche of King Nebkheperure is represented between the wings of a winged snake (Wadjet), which is the protective goddess of the North, whose engraved body is coiled on a papyrus plant symbolic of Lower Egypt (North). Beside the snake, a text contains a wish that the king will receive life and protection forever like Ra.

Below a variation of the usual heraldic symbol of the union of the two lands includes an Asian and a Nubian prisoner, bound and kneeling. The scene is flanked on both sides by two plants: the papyrus and the lotus. The decoration is achieved by the use of granulation, which can clearly be distinguished on the sovereign's wig and the horses' bodies.

GOLD PLAQUE WITH A SCENE REPRESENTING A BULL BEING ATTACKED

Length: 8,5 cm, height: 6 cm

A plaque which shows a hunting scene and an attack on animals, it was among four plates found in the antechamber of the tomb of King Tutankhamun.

The central scene shows the skill of the Egyptian artisans, who have represented the movement of the animals in a natural and very elegant way, something that shows the influence of the art of the Aten period and the idea of a love of nature.

This scene depicts a large bull with a spotted body, his neck surrounded by small disk. It is being attacked by wild animals, a large spotted leopard and a large lion, represented in a very detailed manner. The empty space between the three animals is filled with desert plants.

At either end of the plaque, two ibex are grazing peacefully, desert plants are represented in fine detail.

The plaque is made of reddish gold and the decoration is done in granulation. The bodies of the animals are surrounded by a form of small beads, and the frame bordering the plate and separating the central scene from the two ends, is formed of gold disks.

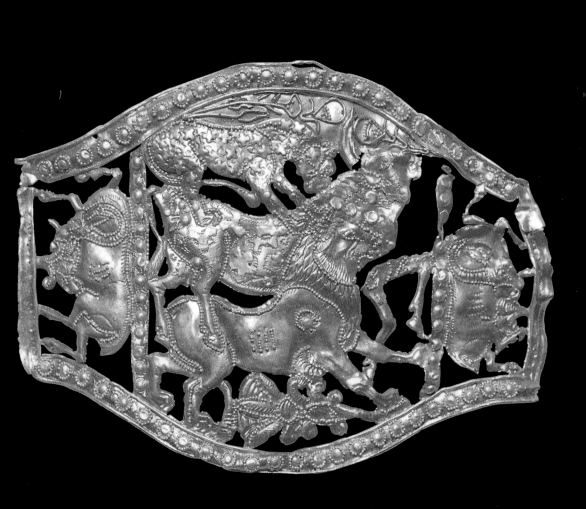

GOLD PLAQUE REPRESENTING THE KING ON HIS THRONE

Length: 8 cm, height 7 cm

The plaque in reddish gold was found in a chest inside the tomb of King Tutankhamun. The main part of the plaque is a rectangular chapel surmounted by a number of friezes, a frieze of *uræi* with solar disks and geometric ones formed of squares.

Beneath this chapel, King Tutankhamun is sitting on a throne with a high back and high sloping armrests decorated with sphinxes and vultures, the decoration is incised. The king's throne bears the *sematawy* symbol of the unification of Egypt, formed by the two heraldic plants: lotuses and papyrus, which are knotted around the central part.

The king is wearing the blue *khepresh* crown of war, a long, transparent robe that reveals the details of his body and a long collar with granulated decoration around his neck. One of his hands is raised to chest level and holds two sceptres, the *heka* crook and the *nekhekh* flail, the other hand resting on his knee holds the *ankh* sign, which means life.

A ribbon floats at his neck and in front of his face, a vulture Nekhbet, spreads its wings holding in its talons the *shen* sign (eternity). Beneath the vulture is engraved text containing a wish for protection and the cartouche of (Nebkheperure).

The chapel rests on a basket with a diamond meaning *sed* or jubilee incised in the centre. It is flanked by two representations, which convey the festive celebrations of King Tutankhamun.

In front of the chapel, stands a lunar spirit in the form of a thin man, on his head he is wearing a headdress resembling a *nemes* topped by a disk and a lunar crescent, he has a curled beard, a necklace comprising several rows that hides the chest, and a short half pleated kilt. The spirit holds a tray topped by a sphinx wearing the double crown and a straight beard, it is the god Atum as we learn from the text in front of his face.

Beneath the tray, symbols of festivals and jubilees are carried by Heh the god of eternity, represented in the form of a man with his arms raised, in his hands is the *renpet* sign of years. This god is placed on the *sed* or jubilee basket. Behind the chapel, the goddess Maat in the shape of a winged woman is standing with the feather of justice on her head. She is spreading her wings around the king to protect him and holding in her hands the *renpet* sign of years, ending at the bottom in the body of a tadpole surmounting the *shen* sign symbol of a million years. Between the goddess's wings, the king's cartouche (Nebkheperure) is placed on the *neb* sign, which means all.

This piece commemorates one of the celebrations of King Tutankhamun, the monarch is represented wearing ceremonial robes, the *sed* sign repeated several times, the god Heh with the symbol of years placed on the *sed* sign, with the presentation of the divinities Atum and Maat,

BRACELET WITH THREE SCARABS

Length: 17.6 cm, height: 4.3 cm

A great number of bracelets were discovered in the chests and the mummy strips of King Tutankhamun, seven on his right arm and six on his left, distributed between the wrists and shoulders.

These bracelets did not play a funerary role but included the forms of divinities and the most important amulets like the *wadjet* eye, the *kheper* scarab, the *uræus* and the vulture.

These ornaments could have been worn by Tutankhamun during his lifetime so Carter believed. The sovereign probably decided to wear the greatest number in the tomb, which explains the abundance of jewellery on the mummy. This bracelet was on the king's left arm; it is an example of the arrangement of magic protection and a masterly use of colour with an imaginative touch for the clasp. The bracelet does not have a central component; it represents a group of elements repeated three times, they are:

1. A scarab of lapis lazuli set in gold positioned on a base of solid gold, symbolizing the *kheper* sun and regeneration,.

2. Three important symbols, which are the *neb* sign (totality) in light blue glass paste surmounted by two elements, *nefer* (beauty), and the *uræus* surmounted by a cornelian solar disk set in gold.

This group conveys to us the wish: (All beauty, protection, regeneration and existence).

Six rows of gold and blue glass paste beads form the top and bottom of the bracelet, they are held by a sliding clasp in the shape of a grasshopper with gold legs, whose body is inlaid with blue glass paste. Close to the grasshopper's head is an engraved rosette.

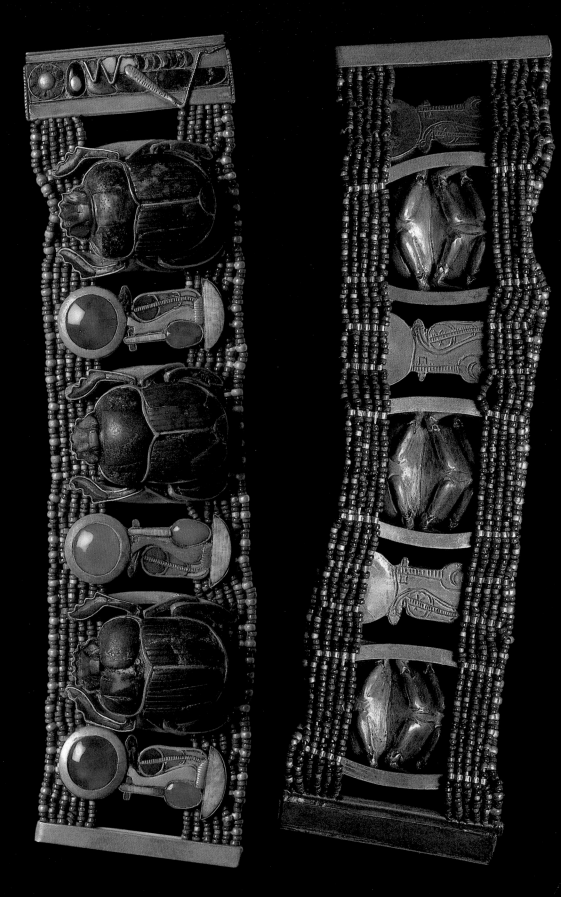

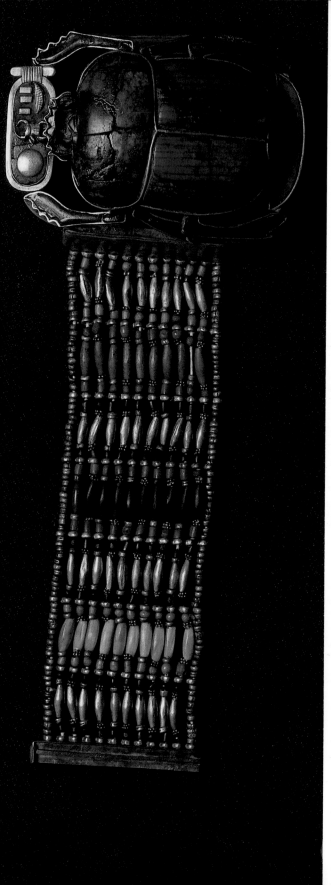

BRACELET WITH SCARAB CLASP

Length: 15,8 cm, height of scarab: 6,6 cm

This bracelet was called a wristband bracelet by Carter and it differs from the other kinds of bracelet which are rigid, being equipped with a hinge and provided with a hook for the clasp.

This bracelet is composed of several rows of beads held in place by long pins and a final element, which generally represents the central part of the bracelet reminding us of a watch.

Three bracelets were discovered in the cartouche-shaped chest, they seem to have been worn by the king during his lifetime. One was rigid and the other two were flexible.

The central part of the bracelet is composed of a decorative motif of a lapis lazuli scarab, composed of several pieces of cloisonné work set in gold and fixed to a gold plate. The front legs of the scarab which usually hold a solar disk, here hold the king's gold cartouche giving us the name Nebkheperure on a ground of blue glass paste.

The bracelet is composed of ten rows of gold, electrum, blue glass paste, lapis lazuli and calcite beads. Eight long gold beads give rigidity to the bracelet by dividing the rows into seven sections. A solid gold clasp fits into a clip placed on one side of the scarab to ensure the closure of the piece.

BRACELET WITH LAPIS LAZULI CENTREPIECE

Length: 16 cm, height: 4.2 cm

This bracelet is simply decorative and does not carry any religious or funerary symbol as does the remainder of the jewellery. It shows traces of wear, which proves it was worn by the sovereign. The bracelet is very flexible and is held in place by a sliding bar.

The piece is composed of a round central part in the form of a lapis lazuli disk speckled with brown, decorated with a double circular pattern in gold worked in a granular pattern.

The external circle is composed of triangular motifs, whereas the interior one is made up of bosses encircled by granules. This same decorative motif is repeated on the solid gold side bars bordering the disk, which at the same time attach it to ten rows of barrel-shaped gold beads separated by small round beads also in gold on each side.

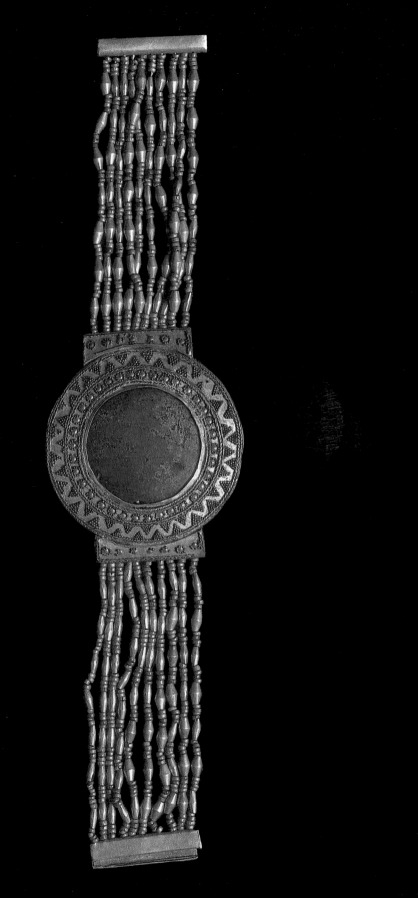

PECTORAL WITH THE GODDESS NUT

Height: 12.6 cm, width: 14.3 cm

The shape of this piece of jewellery is unusual; it was discovered in the *naos* on which the figure of Anubis is resting. Manufactured in solid gold, this ornament is distinguished from other pectorals in the tomb by two eyelets which are not on the upper part but on the right and left sides; this pectoral was probably used as a belt. This part has a frieze of palm tree leaves on its upper side, but on the three other sides is a simple frieze decorated with inlaid squares of cornelian and blue and red glass paste.

On the central part of the pectoral, the goddess Nut, the goddess of the sky (Great in power) is standing in profile, with outstretched arms, furnished with spread wings, whose curved ends clasp the two cartouches containing the names of Tutankhamun.

The goddess wears a close fitting dress with two shoulder straps, trimmed with rosettes; her face, arms, her chest beneath the straps and her feet are inlaid with turquoise. The wig, collar and wings are inlaid with multi-coloured glass paste, dark blue for the wig, red and blue for the collar.

A religious text of eight lines of hieroglyphics engraved on the lapel, tells us that Nut is declaring she opens her wings for her son the Pharaoh Nebkheperure, and extends her wings above the beauty of the sovereign Tutankhamun of Heliopolis, she protects his body like the god Ra.

214

PECTORAL IN A FALCON SHAPE

A pectoral that is simple but of an infinite beauty, which resembles the pectoral of the goddess Nekhbet. It is in the shape of a falcon or the Horus god, one of the important gods of the Egyptian pantheon. The falcon's spread wings curve upwards, it wears a solar disk on the head, which is turned to one side. Its feet are of solid gold and hold in their claws the *shen* signs, symbols of eternity. Between the lower part of the wings and the legs, the *ankh* sign, which means life is attached, it is inlaid with dark blue glass paste.

The details of the head, face and feet are done in a very delicate manner. The shape of the tail feathers differs from those of the body and wings. The inlay of the figure of the god is carried out using a fine technique of sections, filled with glass paste and semi-precious stones of turquoise blue, dark blue and red.

PECTORAL DECORATED WITH A SCARAB AND ISIS AND NEPHTYS

Height: 16 cm, width; 24.4 cm

A form of pectoral, which was repeated several times in the jewellery of Tutankhamun, it contains the representation of an important divinity: the god Kheper, the scarab, one of the symbols of the sun at dawn. The scarab is surrounded by two very active and important goddesses in the Egyptian pantheon, Isis and Nephtys, the two mourning sisters,

This pectoral was found in the Anubis *naos*, it is rectangular and surrounded by a row of blue, yellow and red squares. The pectoral is provided with two eyelets on the right and left-hand sides. The upper part is decorated with two floral friezes with inlays in blue, red and yellow, in something approaching a *khekeru* shape.

The centre of the pectoral is occupied by a heart scarab, generally present in royal or private tombs, placed on the mummy of the deceased above the heart. This scarab is surmounted by a cornelian solar disk with two small snakes hanging from its two sides; it is fashioned in a stone of a green colour and on its inner side, Text 30B of the Book of the Dead is engraved.

The scarab is integrated into the pectoral but is supported by the hands of the two goddesses Isis and Nephtys, who crouch on its right and its left wearing their emblems on their heads, the throne of Isis and the house of Nephtys. The two goddesses are wearing the *afnit*, a headdress in which all the hair is gathered together ending in a ribbon, which hangs down the back. Around the neck, a red and blue collar hides part of the left arm, which supports the scarab.

Isis and Nephtys wear gold bracelets around the hand and on the forearm. Their bodies and faces are inlaid with turquoise. The two goddesses wear the same dress, trimmed with a net motif formed of glass cut out and fitted, but separated by balls and rosettes in very fine gold leaf. The area in front of each goddess's face is occupied by one of the two cartouches of King Tutankhamun, each surmounted by a solar disk inlaid with cornelian.

PECTORAL DECORATED WITH A SCARAB BORDERED BY URÆI

Height: 7.8 cm, width: 8.7 cm

This pectoral was found in the marquetry chest in the treasury and counts among one of the extraordinary pieces in the tomb, thanks to the quality of the execution and the materials employed which are: a gold base, lapis lazuli for the scarab, turquoise and cornelian for the inlays.

The centre of the pectoral is occupied by a large scarab, which is Kheper representing the sun god at dawn, made from lapis lazuli. The artist has depicted the smallest details, the head and the mandibles with which the beetle holds not a ball or a solar disk, but a royal cartouche containing the name of Pharaoh Nebkheperure with the title: (*setepenre*) which means (Chosen of Ra). Between the scarab's back legs is the *shen* symbol of eternity made from turquoise and cornelian.

The beetle is bordered by two *uræi* suspended on the cartouche and surmounted each by a solar disk of cornelian encircled with gold. The very fine details of their bodies are made of gold and coloured glass paste; their heads and throats are delicately cut and inlaid with lapis lazuli and cornelian.

The lower edge of the beetle is very clear cut and is inlaid with glass paste and calcite. The bottom face of the scarab presents the same carved motif engraved in gold; the back shows the joins of the glass paste pieces, and parts of the belly; the forenames registered on the back are followed by two different epithets (Sovereign of truth, the image of Ra).

The backs of the solar disks are provided with eyelets with three openings in which wire remains were found.

PECTORAL DECORATED WITH THE WINGED VULTURE OF NUT

Height: 12.1 cm, width: 17.2 cm

Pectoral found in the Anubis *naos*; it is rectangular having the shape of a sacred building with two eyelets or fasteners on the two upper extremities, each provided with three holes to take as many rows of beads. The pectoral has two friezes of decoration with palm tree leaves and flowers, inlaid with glass paste coloured red, blue, turquoise and yellow. The three other borders of the pectoral are encircled by squares of red and blue glass paste.

The goddess depicted on the pectoral is the vulture Nekhbet, the protective divinity of Upper Egypt, however the hieroglyphic signs above the head identify her as Nut, goddess of the sky, which shows that the vulture here is the image of the goddess Nut and not Nekhbet.

She is represented looking to one side, the two wings are spread out and their ends curve towards the bottom, the beak is inlaid with turquoise, as for the body and wings they are inlaid with glass paste in blue, turquoise blue and red; the two feet are of solid gold and the claws hold two *shen* signs, symbol of eternity inlaid with cornelian and turquoise encircled with gold.

The two cartouches of King Tutankhamun contain mistakes, they are reversed and lack the sign of (sovereignty or *heka*), the name on the left was to be Tutankhamun and that on right was to be another; this pectoral probably belonged to someone else but was modified in a crude fashion.

It is thought that this pectoral probably belonged to Akhenaton and contained his names. It was thus a pectoral from the beginning of his reign in Thebes, but it was afterwards for unknown reasons modified for another sovereign, Tutankhamun by changing the names engraved on the cartouche.

PECTORAL OF OSIRIS, ISIS AND NEPHTYS

Height: 15.5 cm, width: 20 cm

A rectangular pectoral made in gold and completely inlaid with turquoise, lapis lazuli, cornelian and coloured glass paste.

The upper part is decorated by two friezes, the first with scales or feathers and the second with flowers. On the right and left of the two extremities of the upper part are two gold eyelets with the representation of a large coiled winged snake and between its wings the *shen* sign of eternity.

This top is divided by two *uraei* surmounted by gilded solar disks, with the bodies inlaid with red and blue glass paste. The other three sides of the pectoral have geometrical motifs inlaid with glass paste.

The scene on the pectoral is a usual one but represents clearly the possibility of wrongly interpreting the characters. In the centre, a mummified figure in profile is wearing an *atef* crown; it is composed of a cone, a solar disk two ram's horns and two feathers. This figure has a long curved beard, its two arms crossed on the chest hold the crook and the flail insignias of royalty; a long red ribbon hangs down the back and around the neck a broad collar covers the shoulders and chest. The head, sceptres and the parts of the crown are made of gold, but the sheath which enfolds the body is of silver.

The text behind this personage describes him as (Lord of Eternity Eternal Lord, Beneficent God, Master of the Sacred Land). It could refer to the god Osiris, but more probably because of the absence of the god's name, it is about the Pharaoh Tutankhamun becoming Osiris after his death. This figure is flanked by a winged snake with the White Crown and a vulture with the White Crown surrounded by two feathers. The snake and the vulture rest on a basket decorated with a checked pattern, which imitates basket weaving; their bodies are inlaid with glass paste. They spread their wings to protect the central figure while holding a *shen* sign in cornelian ringed with turquoise.

In these two representations one recognizes Nekhbet and Wadjet, the two protective goddesses of the Egyptian pharaoh, but the two texts behind the goddesses identify them as Isis and Nephtys. Behind Isis the vulture, the text says: (That she grants protection and life, beneath her like Ra); whereas behind Nephtys the cobra, the text says: (That she gives protection and life).

61946

PECTORAL DECORATED WITH THE SYMBOLS OF THE SUN AND THE MOON

Height: 14,9 cm, width: 14,5 cm

This pectoral is an important religious symbol, very rich in visible and hidden signs; it constitutes an excellent testimony to the skill of the Egyptian jewellers, who had reached a high level of expressing religious concepts into playing the role of amulets.

This piece is very spectacular and was found in the Anubis chest discovered in the treasury.

The central element of this pectoral is a winged scarab made of a very pure translucent chalcedony of an extreme beauty; it symbolizes the sun at dawn, Kheper, who generally comes out of the sand in the morning pushing a solar disk. Here it holds a lunar boat using its two forefeet, inlaid with turquoise in the middle and with gold on the two sides and the extremities carved in the form of a papyrus flower.

A boat on which is posed the left eye of the god Ra, who represents the moon, forms the upper part of the pectoral; it is inlaid with obsidian and calcite and encircled with lapis lazuli. The eyebrow is also inlaid with lapis lazuli, the gap separating it from the eye is filled with a thick sheet of gold leaf. This eye is encircled by two *uræi* each surmounted by a gilded solar disk inlaid with glass paste coloured dark blue, turquoise blue and red.

A gold crescent moon surmounted by a silver lunar disk is posed on the eyebrow. Three characters were welded onto the latter, they represent: the pharaoh standing in profile with a disk and a lunar crescent on his head, flanked by two divinities Thoth the god of wisdom, writing and knowledge with the head of an ibis surmounted by a crescent and a lunar disk, and Rahorakhty with the head of a falcon surmounted by a solar disk. Thoth and Rahorakhty raise their hands to greet the pharaoh.

The lower part of the pectoral offers a more refined symbolism; the scarab has wings and a tail, which are inlaid with cornelian, turquoise and lapis lazuli. The wings are bordered by a thick gold frieze containing six loops through which passed rows of beads. This frieze ends at the bottom in two *uræi* also in gold, each surmounted by a solar disk and inlaid with coloured glass paste.

The back legs of the scarab are those of a vulture holding in its claws the *shen* sign of turquoise and cornelian, and flower stems; in the left claws the fully opened lotus and in the other, the lotus and buds; the lotus represents the plant of Upper Egypt. At the bottom, is a frieze consisting of a garland of cornflowers, lotuses, papyruses and poppies; the inlay of these flowers is of semi-precious stones.

This pectoral is a funerary symbol of the pharaoh; its signs show the stages that the deceased would encounter during his voyage in the afterlife. It is divided into two completely different parts in their signification: the upper part is the lunar boat, the eye of Ra, which is the moon with Thoth, who is also a lunar disk. It is thus death and all that relates to the underworld, as for the lower part it is life, the god Kheper symbolizes the sun at dawn, the snakes with the solar disk and the *she*, which symbolizes eternity; this part represents the wish for rebirth and eternal life, protected by the god Rahorakhty and the *wadjet* amulet of perfection.

PECTORAL WITH LOTUS FRIEZE AND ROYAL FORENAME

Height: 12,5 cm, Width: 13 cm

This piece of jewellery is a large pectoral, very harmonious thanks to the semi-precious stones and glass paste of beautiful colours employed. The religious and funerary symbols are not only decorative but add value to this pectoral; it was found inserted in the strips of the mummy.

The pectoral had one essential role to present the name of Nebkheperure through the scarab and the signs carved in the lower part, but the disproportionately enlarged scarab and two *urœi* dominate the king's name and narrowly confine the two signs, the *ankh* and *wadjet*.

The pectoral is divided into two parts; the centre of the upper part is occupied by the winged lapis lazuli scarab with falcon's wings, inlaid with glass paste, lapis lazuli and cornelian. The wings curve upwards to touch a lunar disk of electrum, a mixture of gold and silver; this disk rests on a lunar crescent. Beneath the scarab, the signs of the plural and basket are engraved in the gold, which together with the scarab write the sovereign's name.

The scarab is protected on both sides by two large *urœi* surmounted by two gilded disks inlaid with coloured glass paste; close by two *wadjet* eyes, symbol of protection and perfection and two *ankh* signs are engraved.

The upper part is based on a frieze of circles of various colours on a gold sheet, as for the lower part it is composed of lotus and papyrus flowers attached to each other by circles. The flowers are inlaid with gold, cornelian and lapis lazuli.

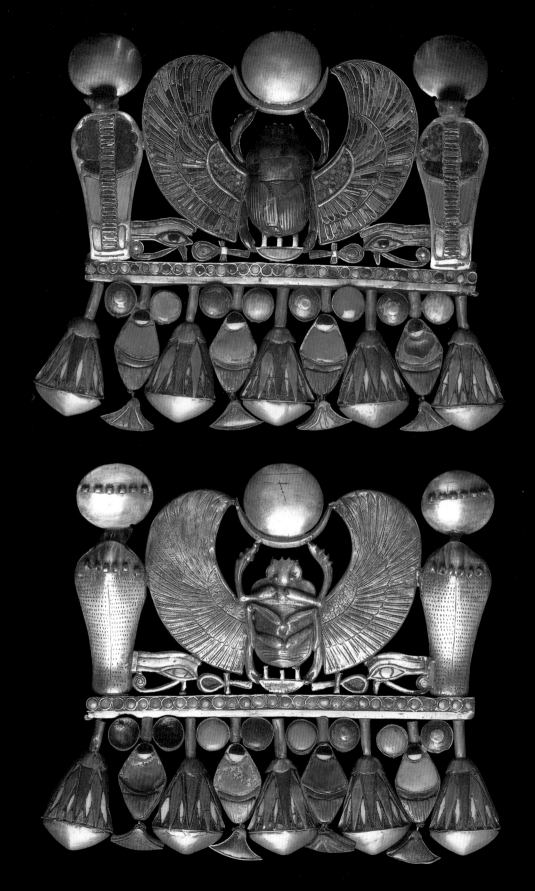

PECTORAL COLLAR WITH VULTURE

Width of the vulture: 11 cm, length of the collar: 25.5 cm

This very simple collar was suspended from the mummy's neck; it is very interesting among the jewellery in the tomb. It shows the animal form of the goddess Nekhbet, protective goddess of the pharaoh in his role as king of Upper Egypt.

The vulture spreads its wings towards the lower part, the two legs are spread apart and the claws hold the *shen* sign, symbol of eternity. The flexible head can be moved and turned; it is made from gold and is delicately worked with a lapis lazuli beak and obsidian eyes.

The decoration of this piece of jewellery is very original, the artist has made gold sections filled with blue glass paste and then fired them to fix the colour. The back is inlaid in the same way as the front. The gold chain attached to this pectoral is rolled.

UNGUENT JAR IN THE SHAPE OF A PROTECTIVE LION

Height 60 cm, width 19.8 cm

This vase is cut from a single piece of calcite; it depicts a lion standing on its hind legs welcoming visitors, it right foreleg raised and its tongue protruding; it stands on a stool with a rectangular top. The upper part of the stool is masked by a broad band decorated with a frieze made up of three bands of colours, the first with blue and white checks, the second with white and yellow checks, in addition to circular shapes of mandrake roots and feathers (khekeru).

From the block of calcite from which the body is cut, emerge the tail, hind legs, mane and a large hieroglyphic sign on which the beast rests its left leg evoking its protection. The animal's mane is a real work of art being assembled from two essential parts; the base coiled at the top and the bottom, and a floral composition painted on a wide form with a blue ground and sorts of bouquets assembled with a lotus flower. This mane was actually the stopper of the unguents, closed by a skin still covered with vestiges of linen fabric.

The ring of hair which frames the mouth, the details of the ears, the animal's claws, the final tuft of the tail, the little rosettes of fur on the shoulders, all these are heightened by the use of a blue black colour.

The nose shows traces of red, which indicate the nostrils, the eyes are encircled in black, the open mouth has eight white ivory fangs and the protruding tongue is painted red; the bored ears of the animal were for gold rings. On the chest, a small panel surmounted by the sign of the sky carries three cartouches, two belonging to the king and one to the queen, containing their usual titles. The contents of this vase could have been fat to produce light, or perfumes used in purification and as remedies against harmful influences, or the unguents necessary for safeguarding the mummy, which could effectively fulfil their role thanks to the magic probably related to Bes, which protected them. This magic is the king himself fighting for his birth, in accordance with the presence of his cartouche on the animal's chest.

GLOSSARY

Aba	A scepter symbolizing the commandant.
Afnit	Scarf covers the hair and attaches on the back. It is similar to the *khat*.
Aker	Two lions seated back to back. They appear in the Book of the Dead and in the mythic texts.
Ankh	Sign of life.
Atef	Crown of the god Osiris flanked by two feathers.
Ba	One of the elements of a person, representing his soul, depicted as a human-headed bird.
Behdet	Ancient name for Edfu city.
Chawap	Wood.
Chen	Sign of eternity, ancient shape of the cartouche.
Deshret	The Red Crown of Lower Egypt.
Djed	A pillar, symbol of stability.
Dwa	A star.
Dwat	The «next world» or the «under world».
Dw	A verb meaning «to grant».
Hedjet	White Crown of Upper Egypt.
Heka	A scepter in the form of a crook, symbol of power.
Hem-neter	The servants of God (priests).
Iaru	Fields representing ancient Egyptian's paradise.
Ib	One of the elements of a person representing his heart, center of the wisdom and thinking.
Ikm	Shield.
Imiut-set-sa	Priests who were probably in charge of all the manual labor inside the temple.
Imy-dwat	The religious book of what is in the next world.
It-neter	The fathers of the god (priests).
Ka	One of the elements of a person, representing his double or the vital force, depicted as two upraised arms.
Keriu-hebet	Priests whose role was to ordain the rituals and to recite out loud the sacred anthems during the rituals.
Khasut	Foreign lands.
Khat	A royal head dress.
Khekeru	Frame representing the tied reeds, which used to form enclosure walls around primitive buildings or was woven over mud brick buildings.
Kheperesh	The Blue Crown often called the war crown.
Khepesh	Short sword.
Kherep	Scepter of authority.
Maat kheru	The deceased, true of voice.
Mendjet	The solar barks during the 12 hours of the day.
Mesketet	The nocturnal solar barks.

Mu	Water.
Neb	Everything.
Nebu	The gold sign.
Nbty	The two ladies, Wadjet and Nekhbet, goddesses of Upper and *bty* Lower Egypt, one of the royal titles.
Nefer	The word beautiful for a man.
Neferet	The word beautiful for a woman.
Nekheb	Ancient name for the city of el-Kab.
Nekhekh	The flagellum scepter, symbol of authority.
Nemes	Royal head dress.
Nsw-biti	king of Upper and Lower Egypt, one of the royal titles.
Niut	City or capital.
Opet	An annual festivity celebrated between the temples of Luxor and Karnak.
Wabu	The pure priests who were taking care of the instruments and the sacred objects of the cult on a daily basis.
Wadj	Papyrus.
Was	Scepter with canine head symbolizing prosperity.
Ouchep	Verb meaning «to answer».
Udjat	A protective amulet representing the eye of the god Horus.
Ouehem	Amulet representing rebirth.
Ouer-kherep-hemat	Masters of art (priests).
Ouer-maou	Visionaries or religious chiefs of Re's clergy in Heliopolis (priests).
Oun	Heliopolis.
Usekh	Broad beads collar.
Ushebtis	Funeral mummy-shaped statues that were placed in the tomb and buried with the deceased.
Pernu	Temple of Lower Egypt during the pre-dynastic period.
Perouer	Primitive temple of Upper Egypt.
Pet	Sky.
Rekhyt	Birds symbolizing subjects.
Renpout	Sign of years.
Routy	Geniuses in the shape of a lion.
Sa	Protective amulet.
Sed	Name of a celebration that takes place every 30 years, symbol of festivity.
Sekhem	A scepter symbolizing power.
Sem	Priests who preside at funeral.
Sema-tawi	Unification of the two lands.
Sene	A board game, the name means «passing game».
Sepat	Nome.
Setepenre	An expression meaning the «elected by god».
Sheneb	The trumpet.

Temehou, Nehesou,	
Restiou, Medjay,	Enemy tribes of the king that were attacking the Egyptian borders.
Tehenou, Sdjetiou,	
Ouaouat, Retenou and the *Amou*	
Thebouy	Sandals of ancient Egyptians.
Tit	The knotted girdle of the goddess Isis.
Uraeus	Frontal cobra protecting the statues of the kings and the gods.

BIBLIOGRAPHY

1. C. Aldred, *New Kingdom Art in Ancient Egypt*, London, 1951.

2. J. Capart, *L'art égyptien, Etude et Histoire*, Vol. I, Bruxelles, 1924.

3. J. Capart, *Tout- Ankh- Amon*, in collaboration of M. Werbrouck, E. Bille de mot, J. Taupin et P. Gilbert, Bruxelles, 1943.

4. H. Carter and A. Mace (Cassell) and Co. Ltd., *The Tomb of Tut- Ankh-Amen*,

Vol. I, London, New York, Toronto and Melbourne, 1923-1926-1927.

Vol. II, with the appendices of D. Derry, A. Lucas, P. Newberry, A. scott, H. Pienderleith, 1927.

Vol. III, with the appendices of D. Derry & A. Lucas, 1933.

5. J. P. Corteggiani, *L'Égypte des pharaons au Musée du Caire*, Paris, 1979, 1986.

6. N.De G. Davies, *The rock tombs of El Amarna,* London, 1903-1908.

7. N.De G. Davies & A. H. Gardiner, *The Tomb of Huy, Viceroy of Nubia in the reign of Tut'ankhamun*, London, 1926.

8. Ch. Desroches-Noblecourt, *Vie et mort d'un pharaon*, Hachette, 1963-1965.

9. V. Dijk Jacobus & M. Eaton-Krauss, *Tutankhamun at Memphis*, MDAIK 42, 1986, 35-41.

10. S. Donadoni, *Le Musée Egyptien, les Musées du monde*, Paris, 1971.

11. E. Drioton, *Le Musée égyptien*, Cairo, 1939.

12. E. Drioton, *Le Musée du Caire, Encyclopédie photographique de l'art,* TEL, Paris, 1949.

13. P. Fox, *Tutankhamun's Treasure,* London, 1951.

14. Frankfort & Pendelebury, *The city of Akhenaton,* Egypt Exploration Society, London, 1923-1951.

15. W. Hayes, *The Scepter of Egypt*, New Kingdom (Vol. II), Cambridge, Mass. 1959.

16. E. Hornung, *Les dieux de l'Egypte. Le un et le multiple*, Paris, 1986.

17. J. Jequier, *A propos des grands lits de Toutankhamon*, Recueil de travaux relatifs à la philologie et à l'archéologie égyptienne et Assyriennes XL, 1923.

18. M. Malaise, *Les scarabés de cœur de l'Égypte ancienne*, Bruxelles, 1978 (MFERE).

19. D. Meeks & Ch. Meeks- Favard, *La vie quotidienne des dieux égyptiens*, Paris 1993.

20. B.G. Ockinga, *New light on Tutankhamun. The tomb of Sennedjem at awlad azzaz*, Sohag, Congress 6, 1991.

21. J. Padro & F. Molina, *Toutankhamon et son temps*, exhibition, Paris, 1967.

22. E. Peet, L. Wooley, B. Gunn, P. Guy & F. Newton, *The city of Akhenaton*, Edited by Egypt Exploration Society in three volumes, Part I, London 1923, Part II, London 1933, Part III, London, 1951.

23. A. Piankoff, *The Shrines of Tut-ankh-Amon,* Edited by N. Rambova, Bollingen Series XL.2, Princeton University Press, 1977.

24. J. Ray, *The parentage of Tutankhamun,* Antiquity 49, 1975.

25. C.N. Reeves, *The complete Tutankhamun*, London, 1990 a.

26. G. Robins, *The proportions of figures in the decoration of the tomb of Tutankhamun (KV 62) and Ay (KV 23),* GM 72, 1984 a.

27. G. Robins, *Two statues from the tomb of Tutankhamun, GM* 71, 1984 a.

28. G. Robins, *The mother of Tutankhamun (2)* , DE 22, 1992.

29. Julia.E. Samson, *Royal inscriptions from Amarna* , (Petrie Collection, UC London), *CdE* 48, 1973.

30. H.D. Shmitz, *A l'ombre de Toutankhamon*, Saqqara, 1990.

31. E. Terrace & H. Fischer, *Treasures of Egyptian art from the Cairo Museum*, London, 1970.

32. M.Tosi, A. Roccati, *Tutankhamun and his time (Tutankhamun, i ivo vremia)*, Moscow, 1976.

33. Cl. Traunecker, *Les dieux de l'Egypte*, Paris 1992, Que sais-je?

34. Cl. Vandersleyen, *Armanismes: le « disque» d'Aton, le « roi asexué»*, CdE 59, 1984, 5-13.

35. Cl. Vandersleyen, *L'iconographie de Toutankhamon et les effigies provenant de sa tombe*, Mél. Wild, 1984-1985, 309-321.

36. Cl. Vandersleyen, *Ankhesenamon et le naos doré* C108, GM 119, 1990a, 127-128.

37. Cl. Vandersleyen, *L'histoire de l'art au service de l'histoire*, Congrés 6, Atti I, 1992a, 629-633.

38. Cl. Vandersleyen, *Royal Figures from Tut'ankhamun's tomb: their Historical Usefulness, after Tut'ankhamun*, 1992a.

39. J. Vandier, *The Overseer of the Treasury Maya: a biographical sketch*, OMRO 70, 1990, 23-28.

40. J. Vandier, *The Symbolism of the Memphite Djed-Pillar*, OMRO 66, 1986b, 7-17.

41. J. Vandier, *Toutankhamon, sa famille, son règne*, Journal des Savants, 1967, 65-91.

42. J. Vercoutter, *Toutankhamon dans les archives hittites*, Istanbul, 1961.

43. The Catalogues of Tutankhamun Exhibitions:

    USA Tutankhamun Treasures 1961-63.

    Japan Tutankhamen exhibition in Japan, 1965-66.

    Paris Toutankhamon et son temps, 1967. Petit palais.

    London Treasures of Tutankhamun, British Museum 1972.

    USSR Temporary exhibition 1974.

    USA & Canada Treasures of Tutankhamun 1976-79.

    Germany Tutanchamun 1980-81.

BIOGRAPHY

Dr. Mey Zaki, is an associate professor at the Faculty of Tourism and Hospitality Management, Helwan University, Cairo, Egypt.

After receiving her BA, she completed her master thesis titled "Foreign divinities in Egypt till the end of the New Kingdom", Cairo, 1996.

In 2001, her doctoral thesis "Religious tendency of the inhabitants of Deir el-Medina and its influence on the iconographic style of their tombs" obtained the best doctoral thesis prize for 2001-2002, from Helwan University.

Dr. Zaki published many articles discussing different subjects such as: the idea of symbolism throughout the New Kingdom; rare scenes from the Middle Kingdom; scenes representing the Oasis in the nobles' tombs of Thebes; dances during festivals; the Goddesses of Deir el-Medina and a detailed study about a new stela dating from the second intermediate period.

She participated in several conferences: "Egyptology" held at Grenoble; "Pharaonic music" organized at Helwan; "Pharaonic Calligraphy" took place in Alexandria, "Folkloric and popular art" arranged by the Supreme Council of Culture in Cairo, in cooperation with the Council of Archeology in Fayoum.

She supervised a wide range of thesis prepared by students from Helwan University and Suez Canal University. She is the author of several books: "Festivals in Ancient Egypt", "The History of the Pharaonic Egypt" and the "Luxor Temple" .

In this book, the writer sheds the light on the history, the art and the Aton religion in Egypt during the period preceding the reign of Tutankhamun, as well as the impressive discovery of his tomb. This work offers an historical, symbolic and artistic study covering a considerable number of artifacts and masterpieces from the collection of Tutankhamun, the child King.